# Signposts For Balance In Love And Work

By Vicki Bennett And Ian Mathieson

**Level 2**
(1300-word)

IBC パブリッシング

# はじめに

　ラダーシリーズは、「はしご（ladder）」を使って一歩一歩上を目指すように、学習者の実力に合わせ、無理なくステップアップできるよう開発された英文リーダーのシリーズです。

　リーディング力をつけるためには、繰り返したくさん読むこと、いわゆる「多読」がもっとも効果的な学習法であると言われています。多読では、「1. 速く 2. 訳さず英語のまま 3. なるべく辞書を使わず」に読むことが大切です。スピードを計るなど、速く読むよう心がけましょう（たとえば TOEIC® テストの音声スピードはおよそ 1 分間に 150 語です）。そして 1 語ずつ訳すのではなく、英語を英語のまま理解するくせをつけるようにします。こうして読み続けるうちに語感がついてきて、だんだんと英語が理解できるようになるのです。まずは、ラダーシリーズの中からあなたのレベルに合った本を選び、少しずつ英文に慣れ親しんでください。たくさんの本を手にとるうちに、英文書がすらすら読めるようになってくるはずです。

## E-CAT

**E**nglish **C**onversational **A**bility **T**est
国際英語会話能力検定

● **E-CATとは…**
英語が話せるようになるための
テストです。インターネット
ベースで、30分であなたの発
話力をチェックします。

www.ecatexam.com

## iTEP

● **iTEP®とは…**
世界各国の企業、政府機関、アメリカの大学
300校以上が、英語能力判定テストとして採用。
オンラインによる90分のテストで文法、リー
ディング、リスニング、ライティング、スピー
キングの5技能をスコア化。iTEP®は、留学、就
職、海外赴任などに必要な、世界に通用する英
語力を総合的に評価する画期的なテストです。

www.itepexamjapan.com

### 《本シリーズの特徴》

- 中学校レベルから中級者レベルまで5段階に分かれています。自分に合ったレベルからスタートしてください。
- クラシックから現代文学、ノンフィクション、ビジネスと幅広いジャンルを扱っています。あなたの興味に合わせてタイトルを選べます。
- 巻末のワードリストで、いつでもどこでも単語の意味を確認できます。レベル1、2では、文中の全ての単語が、レベル3以上は中学校レベル外の単語が掲載されています。
- カバーにヘッドホーンマークのついているタイトルは、オーディオ・サポートがあります。ウェブから購入／ダウンロードし、リスニング教材としても併用できます。

### 《使用語彙について》

レベル1：中学校で学習する単語約1000語

レベル2：レベル1の単語＋使用頻度の高い単語約300語

レベル3：レベル1の単語＋使用頻度の高い単語約600語

レベル4：レベル1の単語＋使用頻度の高い単語約1000語

レベル5：語彙制限なし

*'This book is dedicated to all the souls
who have the courage to love with all their hearts.'*

Vicki Bennett and Ian Mathieson

## 読みはじめる前に

本書で使われている用語です。わからない語は巻末のワードリストで確認しましょう。

- [ ] career
- [ ] opportunity
- [ ] relationship
- [ ] mindset
- [ ] positive
- [ ] signpost

### 名言の著者

**Louise L. Hay**「ルイーズ・L・ヘイ」(生年不明-) アメリカの作家。1976年出版の *Heal Your Body* はセルフヘルプ書の元祖として25カ国語に翻訳され、世界33カ国で読み継がれている。

**William Wordsworth**「ウィリアム・ワーズワース」(1770-1850) イギリス・ロマン派を代表する桂冠詩人。湖水地方の自然美を愛した。

**Eleanor Roosevelt**「エレノア・ルーズヴェルト」(1884-1962) アメリカ合衆国第32代大統領フランクリン・ルーズヴェルト夫人にして、優秀な社会運動家。人種差別問題や女性解放運動に早くから取り組み、国際連合の人権委員会長として世界人権宣言の起草にあたるなど多数の業績を残した。

**Faith Hope**「フェイス・ホープ」(生年不明-) オーストラリアの作家、宣教師。アフリカ在住。

**Colin Tipping**「コリン・ティッピング」(生年不明-) アメリカのベストセラースピリチュアル作家。代表作に *Radical Forgiveness* (1997)。

**Gita Bellin**「ギタ・ベリン」(生年不明-) オーストラリアの形而上学者。数々の一流企業のリーダー研修で講師を務める。

**Marianne Williamson**「マリアンヌ・ウィリアムソン」(1952-) アメリカ、テキサス州生まれのスピリチュアル文学作家。児童文学も手がける。著作に *A Return to Love* (1993) など。

**Ashleigh Brilliant**「アシュレイ・ブリリアント」(1933-) 作家、イラストレーター、警句家。イギリス、ロンドン生まれ。アメリカに拠点を移し、17ワード以内の短い文章にイラストを組み合わせた独自の創作活動 Pot-Shots を続けている。

**Leonardo da Vinci**「レオナルド・ダ・ヴィンチ」(1452-1519) イタリアのルネサンス期を代表する巨匠。画家を本業とするが、建築、科学、医学など多分野で活躍した万能の天才。

**Diane Dreher**「ダイアン・ドレイアー」(生年不明-) アメリカ、サンフランシスコで活躍する作家、ホリスティック療法士、スピリチュアルカウンセラー。著作に *The Tao of Inner Peace* (1990) など。

# Contents

**Introduction** ............................................................... *1*

**Chapter 1. How To Meet The Man Of Your Dreams** ......... *3*
  1. Be Natural, And Meet The Man Of Your Dreams  *4*
  2. Love Yourself First, Then Romance May Come  *5*
  3. Understand What Men Want  *6*
  4. Don't Rush Into A Relationship  *7*
  5. Be Willing To Receive Love  *8*
  6. Do Special Things For Your Partner  *9*
  7. Be Gentle  *10*
  8. Have An Open Heart  *11*
  9. Enjoy The Journey Of Love  *12*

**Chapter 2. You Can Create A Happy Relationship** ......... *13*
  10. Know The Type Of Relationship You Want  *14*
  11. Know The Type Of Man You Want To Marry  *15*
  12. Leave The Past Behind You  *16*
  13. Believe That Every Relationship
      Is A Chance For You To Grow  *17*
  14. Listen Before You Talk  *18*
  15. Plant The Seeds For Being Equal  *19*
  16. Don't Fast-forward Your Life During The Bad Parts  *20*
  17. Revenge Won't Make You Happy  *21*
  18. Respect Values  *22*
  19. Set Rules For Anger  *23*
  20. Be Willing To Be Afraid Sometimes  *24*
  21. Know When A Relationship Is At Its End  *25*
  22. Value Your Past Relationships  *26*
  23. Forgive Quickly  *27*

## Chapter 3. Let's Set Goals For Success ........... 29

24. Set Goals For Yourself  *30*
25. Keep Your Goals In Mind  *31*
26. Use Both Sides Of Your Mind  *32*
27. Look Into The Future  *33*
28. Use This Bedtime Exercise  *34*
29. Excite Your Dreams  *35*
30. Don't Give Up Hope  *36*

## Chapter 4. You Can Have Happy Days ........... 37

31. Have Happy Days  *38*
32. Understand What Is Good About You  *39*
33. Forgive Yourself And Others  *40*
34. Notice What You Do Well  *41*
35. Look At Yourself From The Outside  *42*
36. Learn To Control Your Thoughts  *43*
37. Accept That No One Is Perfect  *44*
38. Understand Anger  *45*
39. Think About Now, Not The Future  *46*
40. Think About Now, Not The Past  *47*
41. Be Less Critical Of Yourself  *48*
42. Laugh Often  *50*

## Chapter 5. Be Happy And Successful At Work ........... 51

43. Talk With Your Fellow Workers Often  *52*
44. Be The Best You Can  *53*
45. Receive Compliments At Work  *54*
46. Speak Out When You Need To  *55*
47. Choose Your Words Carefully  *56*
48. Work Well With Your Business Team  *57*
49. Understand Body Language  *58*

50. Live Life Fully  *59*
51. Know That What You Do For Others May Well Come Back To You  *60*
52. Learn From Your Mistakes  *61*
53. Ask For Help  *62*
54. Believe That Your Actions Are An Influence For Others  *63*
55. Think Creatively  *64*
56. Set Goals For Your Career  *65*
57. Use Dreaming At Work  *66*

## Chapter 6. Create Great Friendships  *67*

58. Accept Love And Kindness  *68*
59. Be Honest In Friendships  *69*
60. Listen To Your Feelings About Other People  *70*
61. Listen To Yourself  *71*
62. Show How You Feel  *72*
63. Find Someone To Listen To You  *73*
64. Don't Pass On Gossip  *74*
65. Be Positive And Generous To Others  *75*
66. Do More Kind Things  *76*
67. Don't Compare Yourself With Others  *77*
68. Like Yourself As You Are  *78*
69. Learn To Deal With Disputes  *79*
70. Find Your Own Style  *80*
71. Make A Difference To Other People  *81*

## Chapter 7. Grow Your Talents  *83*

72. Find Your Talents  *84*
73. Listen To Your Feelings  *85*
74. Do Something Different Every Day  *86*
75. Share Your Passion  *87*
76. Find A New Interest Or Skill  *88*

**Chapter 8. Care For Yourself** ········································ *89*

77. Care For Yourself  *90*
78. Say 'No' When You Need To  *91*
79. Let Yourself Cry Sometimes  *92*
80. Be Careful About What You Read  *93*
81. Turn Off The TV, Turn On Your Music  *94*
82. Clear Out Your Wardrobe  *95*
83. Think Before You Buy: Do You Really Need This?  *96*
84. Like Your Body Now  *97*

**Chapter 9. Make Time For Relaxation** ·························· *99*

85. Make Time For Yourself  *100*
86. Be Calm  *101*
87. Learn To Breathe Deeply  *102*
88. Learn To Relax  *103*
89. Do Often What You Like To Do  *104*

**Chapter 10. Discover How To Be Energetic** ···················· *105*

90. Find Your Favorite Exercises  *106*
91. Eat Right And Well  *107*
92. Care For Your Body  *108*
93. Drink Enough Water  *109*
94. Don't Work Too Many Hours  *110*
95. Keep Your Mind Active  *111*
96. Create Positive Energy  *112*
97. Think About The Things You Want  *113*
98. Choose Positive Words  *114*
99. Be A Person Who Takes Action  *115*
100. Break Through Your Fear  *116*

Postscript ·································································· *117*
Word List ·································································· *118*

# Introduction

This is a special book because it offers two different gifts: the chance to develop your English skills and the opportunity to learn a positive mindset. You can learn simple, strong, and beautiful English by reading the messages from each signpost; these messages will assist you to develop your own positive mindset.

Each of the *Signposts For Balance In Love And Work* will give you valuable ideas and tools to help you to discover your own special talents, to be successful in your career, and to find happy relationships and love.

There are 100 *Signposts For Balance In Love And Work*. Each signpost is like a map for your future, giving you direction and guidance to assist you in your life journey, helping you to create personal achievement and satisfaction.

Each of the 100 signposts contains a message and valuable suggestions. Each can be read and absorbed by itself.

If you want to take control of finding success, love, and happiness in all areas of your life, read through the 100 signposts in this book. Your future success is in your hands.

*Chapter 1*

# How To Meet The Man Of Your Dreams

*'There are people looking for exactly
what you have to offer and
you are being brought together
on the checkerboard of life.'*

Louise L. Hay,
Author

## 1.

# Be Natural,
# And Meet The Man Of Your Dreams

Falling in love is not as easy as it may seem or you may think. If you want to find your life partner, there are two important things to do. First be your natural self and second, do the things you enjoy doing.

If you really are your natural self then you will be able to start off the relationship on a true basis. It is very tiring to live your life with someone and have to pretend to be other than who and what you really are. There is no need to pretend to be happier, more positive, or more energetic than you usually are.

When you do activities which you enjoy—for example, going to the gym, dancing, swimming or playing a sport—you will meet many men.

The good thing about this is that you will get to know each other while you are enjoying something you both love to do.

## 2.

# Love Yourself First, Then Romance May Come

It is natural for you to wish for romance in your life, to want something like you see in the movies or hear stories about. To enjoy romance is very special and wonderful. Every one wishes to have a feeling of being special and loved, to enjoy a time of giving special thought and care to another person and receiving these from another person.

It is important to like yourself as you are, and to value yourself; this will allow you to enjoy the relationship more fully when it grows.

Many people want a relationship to fill an empty space in their lives caused by not feeling loved. First fill that empty space in your life with love of yourself. Then when you find someone to love, you can come into that relationship with self-esteem and strength rather than needing the other person to fill you with their love.

3.

# Understand What Men Want

There are many things about relationships that are not understood well. One of these is what men and women most want from a partner.

Many women think men mostly want sex. But if we are really honest and really listen, we find that most men want a partner to listen to them, and to give and receive gentle friendship. They want a partner to talk with about their experiences, someone who is thoughtful about their needs. They want friendship, romance, and love as well as sex.

Many men think women mostly want to be married, to have a family, and to have a man who will work hard and make money. But if we are really honest and really listen, we find that most women want a partner to listen to them, and to give and receive gentle friendship. They want a partner to talk with about their experiences, someone who is thoughtful about their needs. They want friendship, romance, and love as well as sex.

Most men and most women want much the same things in a relationship. There are differences, of course, but mostly it's the same.

## 4.

## Don't Rush Into A Relationship

When you are coming into a relationship, make the time to get to know the other person better. When you feel that there may be a chance of an important relationship, don't rush into it.

If you try to go forward too quickly, this will sometimes have the wrong effect. It may worry the other person because things are happening too fast. The other person may also want a romantic relationship but may want it to grow more slowly. They may want to get to know you a little at a time.

The other person may also be getting used to their own feelings; their feelings may be new feelings to them.

Think about what you want and how you feel. Take care that you do not let your thoughts and actions pull you ahead of the natural course of the relationship. Remember that romance will play a big part early in the relationship.

5.

# Be Willing To Receive Love

When someone you love offers you a compliment, or tells you that you have done something well, or that you look beautiful, it is important that you listen to their compliments and accept them with openness and love. This is a way this person tells you how much they love you.

Smile and say, 'Thank you.' Show your pleasure at the thoughts and the kindness that comes from them. Accept and believe what this person says to you as mostly it will be real and honest and will build your love together as well as your self-esteem.

## 6.

# Do Special Things For Your Partner

When you think about romance in your life, do you wish for someone else to do something special for you? Are you prepared to think about doing something special for them?

Start by thinking about things that you might do for the other person, things that are different and special. It can be a small thing such as writing a note or an email to them or sending them a card with a sweet message. You could do something for them they were not expecting such as leaving flowers on their desk or buying them their favorite food.

It is also important to do some special and thoughtful things for yourself. You could buy some flowers for your bedroom or buy yourself something you like to read or eat. Remember to do nice things for yourself as well as to care for the special person or partner in your life.

# 7.

# Be Gentle

When your relationship is working well and you are happy and in love with your partner it is easy to become busy with other things and put your partner second.

You can sometimes have too much to do at work or with your family. At such times it is easy to put your relationship and your partner in second place to your work or your family.

This is the time to remember to put some effort into your relationship as this will make the other person feel valued and loved. It will also keep the relationship fresh and interesting.

Remember to be gentle often, to show love, and to be warm, thoughtful, and friendly. Touch your partner often. Hold his hand and look into his eyes, and tell him that you love him. Sometimes be passionate. Tell him that although you are very busy, you think of him often and can always make time for him.

## 8.

# Have An Open Heart

Opening your heart to another person seems like a good idea but the thought can raise fear in you as you may be afraid of being hurt.

How do you become openhearted? Many people don't know how.

Think about where your heart is in your body. Feel the feeling you would feel there if you were looking at the face of a child, or a pet, or a beautiful sunset. It is to feel warm, friendly, trusting. It is to feel that you are clear and strong. It is to feel generous. Feel these feelings. That's how you can feel when you open your heart to another person.

Learn how to take these feelings from your heart into your relationship and gain strength from them.

## 9.

# Enjoy The Journey Of Love

It is not a good idea to spend too much thinking about the future of a relationship, wanting everything in the relationship to become perfect.

To love is to go on a journey. Love is not something that you can make perfect. Over time all loving relationships change and grow; they never stay the same.

There will be lots of ups and downs in every relationship, with much to learn along the way. Enjoy love with an open heart and an open mind; make the most of each day.

Enjoy the journey of love in which you will learn much about yourself and about your husband, boyfriend, or partner.

*Chapter 2*

# You Can Create A Happy Relationship

*'The best portion of a good person's life—
their little nameless, unremembered
acts of kindness and of love.'*

William Wordsworth,
Poet

## 10.

# Know The Type Of Relationship You Want

It is very exciting when it seems that a relationship is starting and growing. For a long time you may have been hoping for a romantic relationship and thinking that one will come your way.

It is too easy to be over-excited at the thought of true love becoming possible for you and to rush in expecting that the relationship will grow just as you thought it might.

Think about the type of relationship you would like. Think about the things you would like to do with that other person. Then, see in your mind a loving and caring relationship which you allow to advance in whatever way it does.

Believe that you deserve a loving and caring relationship before you seek to find it from another person.

## 11.

## Know The Type Of Man You Want To Marry

What are the qualities in the man with whom you will want to spend the rest of your life?

Write down as many qualities you can think of that you would like your future partner to have. For example, how tall would you like him to be, what interests would you like him to have? Would you like him to be kind, caring, and thoughtful? Would you like him to have energy and drive or to be more calm and gentle?

Write down as many things as you can. Some people write a list with over 100 things they would like their partner to have and be. Try doing this; it is a great start to finding the man of your dreams.

You will help yourself to create the possibility of your dream coming true, although you may not find all these qualities in the man you come to love. But in writing the qualities down you will have a much clearer idea of what you want in a man.

## 12.

# Leave The Past Behind You

Many people start a new relationship when they still carry the unhappiness from a past relationship that was not a success.

It is difficult to go forward when you are locked into thinking about the past. It is not fair to judge the new person in your life against a person from the past. Some people hold on to past feelings instead of deciding to get on with their new relationship. Thinking too much about the past can take away your self-esteem.

To judge a person against a past relationship does not give the new relationship a chance to grow and become a success. Leave the past behind and be open to a fresh new relationship.

## 13.

# Believe That Every Relationship Is A Chance For You To Grow

Relationships are always changing. Whether your relationship is new or long-lasting, love is always a test. You can think of a relationship as making it possible for you to learn from others and grow in knowledge and wisdom. Doing so can make a big difference for you.

Every relationship offers chances for you to grow and learn about yourself and about the other person. Don't walk away from unfinished problems; talk about the problems with the other person. Don't be afraid to disagree with the other person. This can help you to find understanding. You will then both gain experience, and understanding.

Trust yourself to talk openly with your partner so you can discover new things about each other, and build a stronger friendship as well as love.

## 14.

# Listen Before You Talk

One of the best ways to have a good relationship is to learn to listen to your partner. Most people do not listen well. They wait for the other person to finish speaking so they can say something in reply.

It is important to be able to speak well, to say clearly what you think, and to have a clear and even voice. However, this is only one half of being able to exchange thoughts and ideas.

The other half is to be a good listener.

When someone else speaks, give them your full interest. Look at them, make eye contact, and show them that you care about what they are saying.

Remember to show respect to the other person by being a good listener.

## 15.

# Plant The Seeds For Being Equal

In any relationship, being equal is important. This means that one person's views or wishes do not take over the other's, that both people have equal parts in the relationship.

This does not mean that things have to be equal all the time. Sometimes one person's wishes are so important that the other person will agree anyway. It is a good sign of a happy relationship when one person can see that the other person's wishes are so important that they will agree to what that person wants.

Over time, however, it is important to keep the relationship equal. If the other person's wishes seem to be more important most of the time then you must be able to talk about your need for a more equal relationship. If one person's wishes take over the other person's, this may destroy the relationship.

Be strong; ask for a more equal relationship right from the start.

## 16.

# Don't Fast-forward Your Life During The Bad Parts

Sometimes when you are unhappy or your life seems difficult or you think that you cannot have the things you desire, you may try to escape from these thoughts or events that are unpleasant. You may want life to hurry up past this unhappy time.

Remember that everything that happens to you is of value to you, especially the things that you wish to fast-forward through your life. Try to understand the messages and meanings of things you don't like or enjoy.

Are there important lessons you might learn from these feelings or events? Are there values which have been tested by them, which you have held firm? Are there practices which you might learn, that will be useful for you in the future?

It is likely that you will learn more from your mistakes, from feeling hurt or sad, than from things that go well and from feeling happy. Welcome the difficult parts; they are part of life.

## 17.

# Revenge Won't Make You Happy

Revenge is about feeling anger or hurt about something that has happened in the past. Sometimes when a person hurts another person or makes them angry, the other person then hurts the first person in return. How does that make things right or better? Now there are two people being hurtful instead of one.

If you continue to hold inside your feelings of anger or hurt about a person or something that has happened in your past, this will build up and come to hurt you and lessen your enjoyment of life.

Thoughts of revenge will keep going around and around in your mind until you stop them from doing so. To break the circle of thinking about revenge, learn from what happened and let go of the past experience. The other person may not even know that something was wrong or may have forgotten all about it.

Let go of old bad feelings about people and live your life fully now, rather than in the past.

## 18.

# Respect Values

There are many values from past history and culture that are useful now. Today's society is very different to the society of your parents and grandparents and many of the 'old' values and ways of doing things don't seem to work in today's society, whether at home or at the work place.

However, there is much that is useful today that comes from the ways of the past. Try to find a way to fit the good things from the past into your life now.

Sometimes your parents or friends may try to use the ways of the past to stop you doing what you feel is right for you now. They may try to make you feel bad for thinking thoughts or doing things that are new and different.

Think about where you learned your values—from your parents, your grandparents, your school, and from your own experience. Consider your own values and beliefs and how you can bring some of the values of the past into your life and join them with your own values.

## 19.

# Set Rules For Anger

People in a relationship need to have some rules about how to talk and act with each other. Sometimes anger will rise. It may be because of things said or done by your partner; it may be about something that does not have anything to do with the other person but something they did reminds you of that feeling of anger from the past.

Talk about this together. When you show anger and talk about it, it will pass.

Here are some valuable rules for saying how you feel when you are angry:
- Don't hit the other person by using your hands (or any part of your body).
- Talk about how you feel.
- Try not to hurt the other person's feelings.
- Show that you are willing to let the anger go.
- Make sure you feel good about yourself afterward.

## 20.

# Be Willing To Be Afraid Sometimes

When there is a big difficulty in a relationship it is normal to become afraid and to want to leave the relationship. Deciding to give someone your love can be a big step for you, which can raise doubts in your mind.

Just take a deep breath and accept that from time to time you will feel afraid and not sure, and accept this as part of your relationship.

Learning to know someone is a happy time at first. Later, when people get to know each other better they may notice things they don't like about each other. This is normal. There is an old saying: 'Love cannot see.'

When this happens, think about what is good and positive about your relationship. Talk with your partner about the things you would like them to change and accept the rest.

## 21.

# Know When A Relationship Is At Its End

How do you know if your relationship with a partner or boyfriend is finished? This is a question you may ask yourself more than once in your lifetime.

It may be that there is little joy or happiness for you. You may have learnt everything you can from this person in this relationship, both negative and positive, and all you are doing is going over the same hurt, the same experiences, without changing or growing. If so, then you have probably been as valuable to each other as you can.

Have the courage to let go of a relationship when you know in your heart it's over. When you know that you cannot learn from or add any more value to that relationship, end it. You know you will feel pain and sadness, but you will get over that. For as long as you stay unhappy in an unhappy relationship, you will continue to hurt yourself as well as the other person.

When you end the relationship, remember that this person has helped you to understand some wonderful things. No one else could have given you those experiences.

## 22.
# Value Your Past Relationships

When a relationship does finish, remember that the end of this relationship is a new beginning for you. Some wonderful new experiences are likely to be ahead of you.

Here are some things you can do to put a relationship behind you and move on with your life:
- Believe you will feel better soon. Even though you may not feel very strong now, know that you will be a stronger, wiser person for having been in that relationship.
- Look at the many positives; you had the courage to try a relationship. Some people lack that courage. You tried; you gave it your best effort.
- Value the time and the experience you had together. You had some fun and happiness, romance and love along the way.

## 23.
# Forgive Quickly

Things will happen in relationships where you will need to forgive the other person for something they have done or said, because what they have done or said is something you are not happy about.

Work through to understand the problem and your feelings. Forgive quickly so you can go forward in your relationship.

Instead of jumping in to judge what has happened and staying unhappy about it, think about the whole story. Think about the value of the overall relationship, not only the issue which has upset you.

Try not to think badly about the other person. You also have created part of the problem you are unhappy about, even if it is only a small part. Forgive yourself for the part you created in the problem and then quickly forgive the other person's part in the problem.

Think of the event as a chance to learn. Start by forgiving your partner. No one can gain any pleasure from being unhappy.

*Chapter 3*

# Let's Set Goals For Success

*'The future belongs to those who believe in the beauty of their dreams.'*

Eleanor Roosevelt,
Feminist

## 24.

# Set Goals For Yourself

To become better at doing things at work or at home, learn to set goals. Write these goals you desire in a notebook.

There are three steps to writing goals in your notebook:
  1. Write what you would like to do better.
  2. Write the date you would like to be better by.
  3. Write what actions you will take now and every day to achieve each goal.

For example, you may want to advance your computer skills. This is what you could write:

Goal     1. I will advance my computer skills. I will learn new programs.

Date     2. By 15th December.

Actions 3. Search for computer skills training on the Internet and start study soon. Set aside time every day to practice my computer skills.

Every week, look at your goals list, add other goals, and praise yourself for the goals you have gained. You will be very happy about how many goals you will reach.

## 25.

# Keep Your Goals In Mind

Once you have written your goals you need to keep them clearly in your mind. View them often to see how you have advanced.

When you have completed a goal, cross it off your list. Think about each goal often to decide whether you still want it.

Here are some actions to help you achieve your goals:
- Read your goals every day to think about whether you still want them.
- Remember what you want to achieve.
- Remember to do some small actions every day to advance your goals.
- Make sure your manner and actions suit your goals.
- Mark the goals you have advanced and cross them off your list; you will feel good about yourself and want to keep trying to advance other goals.

## 26.

# Use Both Sides Of Your Mind

Do you use both sides of your mind to help you to move toward your goals?

You use the right side of your mind to dream, to build pictures and ideas in your mind for the future. This is where future goals and information are stored in your mind.

The left side of your mind is for getting things done, for reason, and for common sense. This part of the mind is good at making lists and working on the actions needed to achieve your goals.

It is important both to dream about your goals and then act to achieve these goals. Using both sides of the mind is very important for making your future goals turn into reality.

## 27.

# Look Into The Future

Once you have decided on your goals, the next step is to see the future as if you have succeeded in advancing your goals.

Keep a clear picture in your mind of the future as if you have already completed your goals. Doing this will help you to advance these goals. Also, when you feel that you are not advancing your goals, to see them in your mind is to plant the seeds for them to grow. This will help you not to give up working on your goals.

When you are going to sleep, close your eyes and think about the future. See the goals you have written on your goals list. Picture them as brightly as you can. Think about the goals you have written down and in your mind see them as if they are real.

## 28.

# Use This Bedtime Exercise

Make yourself comfortable in your bed, close your eyes, see yourself experiencing your future dream. Picture yourself doing what you love to do or would like to do in the future. See yourself having success. Experience the feeling you would feel having completed your goal. The more you can experience this future dreaming the better it will be for you.

Go to sleep with the picture in your mind of what you want to have in the future. You may even dream about it in your sleep and this will help you to believe in it for the future.

It is important to believe in your goals for the future.

## 29.

# Excite Your Dreams

When you have an idea about what you would like for your future, play with that idea in your mind first. Don't stop it before it even begins. Don't let the 'I can't do this' part of your mind start before you have thought about the idea first.

Here are some things you can do to create your personal dreams:
- Think about what you would like to have or be in your life. Make a movie of it in your mind with lots and lots of detail.
- Don't force your dream to be too small. Imagine the best. The courage to dream a big dream makes things happen. Wish the very best for yourself.
- Without any sign or facts, believe that your dreams can come true. Everyone starts their dreams that way. You need to believe in yourself as well as your dreams.

## 30.

# Don't Give Up Hope

Never give up hope; have positive thoughts about your dreams. Keep hoping in your heart you will create your dreams.

Take some small actions every day toward your dreams to help them to happen. It is important that your actions help your dreams to advance.

Having the dream alone is not enough; you have to show to the world, and yourself, that you are able to help that dream along with some actions every day of your life. No matter how big or small each action is, do something toward your dreams every day to help them to come true.

Keep your thoughts positive no matter what is happening around you. Never give up hope. Your dreams are the starting point; without them there is no picture for your future.

## *Chapter 4*

# You Can Have Happy Days

*'It's never too late to have a happy life.'*

Faith Hope,
Author

## 31.

# Have Happy Days

Would you like to have more happy days?

What you think about makes a difference to your feelings. If you think positively, you are more likely to feel happier. What do you think about most of the time? Do you think of yourself in a kind and loving way? Or do you think about yourself as not good enough?

If you want to have more happiness in your life, become better at how you think of yourself.

You 'talk' to yourself in your mind, all day every day. What do you 'talk' to yourself about? This needs to be mostly positive if you want to have a happier life.

Start today. Think of yourself as you would think of your very best friend. Talk to yourself as you would talk to your best friend. It may be difficult at the start but it will become a good habit to use every day.

## 32.

# Understand What Is Good About You

Everyone has much that is good in them. Some people say this is not true; they think that people have little that is good in them. But if you look hard and with care, you will find much goodness in every person you know.

Much of the goodness in you is shared with everyone else. Every day there are many examples in the world of people reaching out to others in trouble or in pain. People open their hearts and help others, and this brings humankind together.

This goodness in you is gentle. It is easily broken and you must care for it and treat it with respect.

## 33.

# Forgive Yourself And Others

Forgive yourself for all your past mistakes, for all the wrong or hurtful things you have done or said in the past. You are not alone; everyone has done or said wrong or unkind things.

To be better in future, it is important to forgive yourself for the past things you have done or said, then get on with your life and set goals for future actions.

Try to forgive others too for all the unkind, hurtful things they've said or done to you; they have weak moments also. Like you, that was the best they could do at the time, so forgive them. No one is perfect, you or others.

Forgiving is a very gentle, kind skill to develop.

## 34.

# Notice What You Do Well

Everyone can do many things well but some people just think about the things you don't do well.

Be kind to yourself. Think about the many things you do well right now.

Here is a list of some of the good things that you may already do. Circle all the things you do well:

| | | |
|---|---|---|
| good listener | good cook | believe in myself |
| fun | laugh easily | delightful |
| giving | good | caring |
| helpful | pleasant | kind |
| friendly | openhearted | loving |
| good leader | full of hope | warm |

You can write other good things that are not on the list above.

When you start to notice what you do that is good you will feel good about yourself and you will do more of those good things. Praise yourself a little for those things you do very well.

## 35.

# Look At Yourself From The Outside

When you think about yourself objectively—your values and thoughts, and how you act—you help to clarify your course and future actions.

It is of value to look at yourself from time to time, as if you were looking at another person. Would you like yourself if you were another person? Would you tell yourself to change some parts of you? Perhaps to dress differently or to stand up straight, or to learn a new skill, or to speak more clearly, or to be more gentle and caring?

From time to time, it is good to stand outside of yourself and have a careful look at yourself. Think with care about you and what you like about yourself, and what you would want to change.

This may lead you to decide to change some part of your appearance, your actions, or your beliefs. It may guide you to make some goals for your future.

## 36.

# Learn To Control Your Thoughts

You are in charge of most of the conditions in your life.

Many people blame and judge everything and everybody except themselves for all the bad things that happen in their lives. They do not stop to think that they have added to these events in some way.

Accept that your thoughts and actions have made your life what it is right now. Don't blame everything and everybody for what your life is like. Take charge of the things you have done. Fix the things you are able to fix and make changes for the future so you can create the future you would like for yourself.

## 37.

# Accept That No One Is Perfect

Don't think that you can ever be a perfect person. Many people never really start living their lives because they would like to be perfect and they are waiting for everything to be exactly right. No one is ever perfect. Start living your life fully now; don't wait.

People who want things to be perfect but find that they are not can experience sadness, worry, and stress. Often, people who want perfection may even get less enjoyment than others.

Being perfect is a daydream. It is much harder than doing things the best you can. Trying to be perfect is trying to do things that are not even possible.

Decide on small acts you can do today to do things well, not perfectly.

## 38.

# Understand Anger

Every one gets angry sometimes. Learn to talk about how you feel when you are angry; this will help you to move past the feelings you are feeling. If you don't move past these feelings, the anger inside you will continue to make you feel bad.

Anger is honorable; it comes up to show us how we feel about something at the time.

To cover up your anger with soft words or no words— is that really the best thing to do?

We sometimes think that we are caring for ourselves by not showing anger but we can end up feeling bad as a result and that is not good for us.

When you say how you feel, other people will value you because you have the courage to speak out.

Speak out about any anger you feel and respect yourself when you do so. This is necessary for you to pass through those feelings of anger, and then return to your usual self.

## 39.

# Think About Now, Not The Future

Some people think too much about the past or too much about the future and they forget that now is a great time to be glad and happy about.

Stop right now and look around you; you are a person sitting reading this book, happy. Why would you want more than you have in this moment?

If you live totally now, life is a lot more fun. When you plan too much for the future or worry too much about what happened in the past, you are likely to feel helpless.

If you live in the now, in this moment, then there is very little fear or worry.

## 40.

# Think About Now, Not The Past

Things from the past are important to you, as they make up part of what you are today. Many of the things you remember from your past are good to remember; they are happy, and please you. However, some of the things you remember from the past can make you unhappy, hurt, or sad.

It is not healthy if you spend too much time remembering unhappy past events and feelings. Try not to spend too much time thinking about your past actions and feelings. Try to think about what is happening to you today, right now.

It is important to have some goals for the future and to think about them, but most of your thinking should be about what you are doing now and what you are going to do tomorrow.

## 41.

# Be Less Critical Of Yourself

Don't talk badly about yourself. Most of what you do and what happens around you is positive and good. Your self talk, even about yourself, needs to be mostly positive and good, too.

Negative self talk goes like this:

'My face is ugly.'

'I'm fat.'

'If only I could find a wonderful boyfriend I would be happy.'

'It's his/her fault that I'm unhappy.'

'No one ever thinks about me.'

'I can't do that.'

'I don't have a choice.'

'I'm hopeless; I'll never get through school or university.'

'I hate myself; everyone hates me.'

'I hate my family.'

Positive self talk goes like this:

'I'm beautiful.'

'Everything will be fine.'

'Be patient.'

'Look on the positive side.'

'I'm not listening to these bad thoughts any more.'

'I'm good enough now.'

'I will get through school/university.'

'I will not worry now.'
'I'm going to treat myself well today.'
'I can do this.'

Watch your self talk; keep it mostly positive.

## 42.

# Laugh Often

Are you too serious about your life? Do you let yourself be happy and full of fun often enough? Don't be afraid to settle down, feel easy and open, and laugh.

Every time you laugh you experience a natural feeling of well-being. This helps you to feel well and have a healthy body.

When you have had a good laugh it helps you to feel better about yourself. Smile now and feel how your face feels better from a simple smile.

Be serious when you need to be, but stop being such a serious person all the time. Find ways to laugh more and have more fun.

*Chapter 5*

# Be Happy And Successful At Work

*'Ask for help.
Tell life what you want,
then get out of the way and let it happen.'*

Colin Tipping,
Lecturer

## 43.

# Talk With Your Fellow Workers Often

A key to success in your workplace is to notice the good things your fellow workers are doing in the workplace every day. At least eighty percent of what your fellow workers say and do is good and of value, so at least eighty percent of your talk and advice to them needs to be positive and good. This will build good relationships and make good business.

Sometimes it is not easy to notice the good in your fellow workers, especially if they have made mistakes in the past. Everyone makes mistakes; making mistakes is how we learn to do things better.

If you really wish to have success in your career, you must talk with your fellow workers in a positive and good way most of the time. This will help both them and you to become more valuable in your business life.

## 44.

# Be The Best You Can

When you wish too much for praise from your fellow workers, you will feel upset and sad if you do not receive it. Do not wish for this from them. Instead, try to be the best you can be in your job. When you try to please other people just to be praised you may end up pleasing no one; neither that person, nor yourself.

You are in your work because you have skills and know how to do your job. Trust that you are the best person for that job and go about your work looking for ways to be better.

You can improve one small thing a day, every day.

## 45.

# Receive Compliments At Work

Receive with pleasure any compliments that are given to you at work; it is a sign of a wise and positive business person. Don't think 'Why are they saying that?' or 'What do they really want?' or 'Do they really mean it?'

Everyone is worthy of positive compliments. When you can receive a compliment with pleasure it is a sign that you value yourself. It may be difficult for you to accept compliments with pleasure at first but with practice you will learn to do this.

Every time someone gives you a compliment, simply receive it with pleasure. You will feel better about yourself and about that person. You can never guess why a person makes a compliment. Simply accept it and say 'Thank you.'

## 46.

# Speak Out When You Need To

When something happens at your workplace that you are not happy about and you don't say anything about it, you may feel worse if you didn't speak your own thoughts. Someone may have wronged you or spoken badly about you or acted badly.

Speaking out honestly from your viewpoint is a good thing to do but it takes courage and practice.

Here are some steps you can take to speak out honestly:
- Be sure about the facts first, so you can be sure you are talking about what really happened.
- Speak to the person who it is about.
- Say how you feel about it.
- Speak to them from your heart.
- Offer some positive action.
- Don't feel bad or guilty or worried about speaking out.

When you speak out honestly you will feel good about yourself and other people will respect you more.

## 47.

# Choose Your Words Carefully

Think about the words you use when you talk about your life. Think about whether you are mostly positive or negative. Think about how your choice of words will sound to other people. You are able to choose the words you use.

Here are some different ways of speaking about events in your life:

| **Negative words** | **Positive words** |
| --- | --- |
| There is nothing I can do. | I can find other ways of doing this. |
| That is just the way I am. | I can do this. |
| She/he makes me so mad. | I can choose the way I feel and how I react. |
| They won't let me do this. | I can find a way to do this. |
| I have to do that. | I can choose the way I do that. |
| I'm hopeless. | I'm learning. |
| I can't. | I can try. |
| I must. | I prefer. |
| If only. | I will. |

Choose positive words whenever possible.

## 48.

# Work Well With Your Business Team

How much better could you be if you worked well with your fellow team members? How much more could you gain if you learned to share information? How much more could you work together and help your team members?

Working well with your team is a very bright thing to do; doing so will help you to enjoy your work and advance your career.

This is not always easy to do as some of your colleagues may be difficult to work with. Start by looking for the things they do well and see those things rather than any mistakes they make.

When you become more successful in working well with your fellow workers, you will find everything becomes easier and better for you.

## 49.

# Understand Body Language

Body language is how you sit or stand; how you hold and move your body, face, arms, and legs when you are speaking with another person. When you have clear and positive body language, what you say will be accepted more readily by the person who is listening.

Positive body language counts for about seventy-five percent of the complete messages you give to other people; it is more important than the words you use.

When you use positive body language, look directly at the other person, and give them your full interest. Your eye contact is good, your arms and legs are not crossed and your shoulders and body are straight.

Show people that it is not just in your words but also in your body language that you care about what they are saying.

Good body language builds trust between people.

## 50.

# Live Life Fully

When you are at work, do you waste too much time thinking about the past and all the things you could have done better or made more successful? Or do you waste too much time thinking about the future and what you would like for the future?

Some of us can spend too much time thinking about the future or thinking about the past, wishing the present were different from what it is.

When you live mostly in the present moment you live your life more fully. You notice all of the wonderful people and deeds and things that are around you.

Life is best lived in the present; now, not in the past or future.

## 51.

# Know That What You Do For Others May Well Come Back To You

This is a truth about life: 'Life is like a circle, what you do for others, will come back to you in some way.' How you talk with people and how you act toward them makes a difference to them and to you.

A kind or thoughtful act toward another person may not be returned from the same person but if you are patient, your life will always bring good things back to you because of your practice of doing good things for others.

When you talk with others clearly, warmly, and with energy you make it easy for them to understand you, learn from you, and succeed in working with you. This is a very positive way to change the way other people treat you.

## 52.

# Learn From Your Mistakes

You learn much about what to do and what not to do from your mistakes. No one really likes to make mistakes, especially at work because no one likes to look as if they don't know what they are doing. However, there is value in making mistakes.

You sometimes do some things badly at first but with practice you will learn to do them well so accept mistakes as helping you to learn.

It is probable that you will learn more when you have tried something and it did not succeed, as when it did. To see another person make a mistake does not give you the same understanding as making the same mistake yourself.

You learn when you have experienced the mistake for yourself, when you feel happy or sad about your own experience.

Try to learn quickly and be kind to yourself when you make a mistake.

## 53.

# Ask For Help

Many people are afraid to ask for help when they need to know something or need more information. They don't want to seem as if they don't know what they think they should know. They go through life being shy or afraid to ask for help.

It is strength to be able to ask for help when you need it. Asking for help is not showing that you have failed. It shows that you are willing to learn and change. If you don't ask for help when you need it, it will be hard to learn more information or grow as a person.

Most people will respect you because you are able to ask for help or information, and will be willing to help you as much as they are able.

## 54.

# Believe That Your Actions Are An Influence For Others

People in the workplace may think of you as a special person and want to learn from you. This may surprise you but for some of your coworkers you may have such a strong, positive influence. Being liked and valued in the workplace often happens and is a very special thing. Be willing to help others with information when asked.

It is important for you to show to others actions and values which are steady and uniform. To be a strong influence for other people you need to set some goals for any values you would like to improve. Take some action to make these goals happen every day.

It is an honor to be seen as a person with values and as someone others can learn from.

## 55.

# Think Creatively

Everyone is able to think in a creative manner. Creative thinking is dreaming while you are not sleeping. It is to allow your mind to play with ideas which you have not thought of before, without judging those ideas.

Thinking in this way from time to time will be of value to you as you will be able to think of new ideas, and find answers to problems.

Be ready to accept thoughts which surprise you. Creative thinking is to help unexpected and surprising new ideas to come into your mind.

Try to use creative thinking in your work; it may help you to be better at your job.

You will need courage to put your creative ideas into practice. Find that courage and act on your creative thoughts.

## 56.

# Set Goals For Your Career

Whether or not you are happy in your career now, there is value for you to have a dream for your future career.

Write your career goals in a notebook and read these goals often. You may decide that you need different skills. You may consider changing to a new job.

Then do something every day toward making the goals come true.

Believe in yourself and know that you can have the career you dream of. Believe that this career goal will happen.

See your future career in your dreams as you would like it to be. Believe in your future career goals even though they may seem beyond your reach right now.

## 57.

# Use Dreaming At Work

When you dream about the things you would like to be able to do in your job or have at work, you set your mind into action to think about and create the future as you would like it to be. When you think about and clearly see your future, your mind takes up the thoughts and works toward creating the dream.

This is how it works. Take a break at work, find a quiet place, and take time to picture in your mind the positive future you desire for your work life. Do this for five to ten minutes every day. Imagine what you would like to do, be, have, see, enjoy and then see it in your mind's eye.

Let your mind picture your job or work dreams. See your dreams as brightly as possible. After you have done this you will return to work happier and more positive.

*Chapter 6*

# Create Great Friendships

*'Everything I do and say with anyone
makes a difference.'*

Gita Bellin,
Metaphysician

## 58.

# Accept Love And Kindness

Accept love or kindness with an open heart. For many people it is not easy to accept kindness if you are not used to it.

Don't weigh up whether the person being kind is being honest or not. This is not up to you to know. Just accept their love and kindness warmly, without feeling negative or unkind.

How can you ever know if someone is being honest or not in their kindness? The world can offer so little kindness that it is valuable to accept what comes your way when it comes your way.

You will never be able to work out if the person really means it or not. Just take the kindness into your heart and feel it and accept it. You will be the better for it.

## 59.

# Be Honest In Friendships

Make some rules for yourself about what you will and won't accept in a friendship.

Be open with others about who you are and what you believe. Set rules for yourself about how you wish others to act toward you. When you feel another person has broken your rules, tell them what they have done and how you feel. Think about what you want and what you expect from a friend.

Tell the other person how you feel even if it is difficult to do so. Telling the truth can be difficult because you may think that doing so will make the other person not like you. If you want to build a strong friendship with someone it is important to be able to talk to them about your rules and values and what friendship means to you.

## 60.

# Listen To Your Feelings About Other People

Sometimes you may have a feeling that something is not right about a person and what they are doing. If you have a strange feeling that something is not quite right about a person, listen to it. Your 'something is not quite right about this person' feeling is usually very true.

If you feel that someone is not being honest or true in the way they are acting toward you, ask yourself these questions:
- Do they lie?
- Do they often talk about how other people have acted badly toward them in the past?
- Do they not want to share you with other friends?
- Do they say bad things about other people a lot of the time?
- Do they not do what they said they would do?
- Do they blame other people for their problems?

If you see any of the above, trust your feelings. Have the courage to end the friendship and make new friends about whom you can have better feelings.

## 61.

# Listen To Yourself

It is very important to listen to others when they talk to you. It is equally important to consider your own thoughts; do not accept the views of others without considering your own wishes.

Most of the time other people are likely to say more about what they think and what they would do and not take your thoughts and wishes into consideration.

Let's say you tell your friend that you want to leave your job and get another job. For them, it may seem to be the worst choice in the world and they will tell you about their fears.

They might say things such as, 'You are doing the wrong thing, you will be sorry', or 'You don't know what you are doing', but what they really mean to say is, 'The thought of doing that makes me feel uneasy because I couldn't do it myself, so don't talk with me about doing it.'

They are giving you their own point of view. It is you who makes decisions for you, not your friends. Listen to friends, but always decide for yourself.

## 62.

# Show How You Feel

You may have been told not to talk about how you feel; that you should act as if you have no emotion or feelings; that you must not show your anger, hurt, or any other true feeling at any time.

In your notebook write down how you feel right now. Some people are not very good at telling other people about their feelings, but it can be a great help to write them down on paper. Unless you want to, you don't have to show this to anyone.

A young woman told us that, for her, writing her feelings on paper was 'Like talking to a friend I can confide in and tell all my feelings to.'

It is healthy to show your emotions to other people.

## 63.

# Find Someone To Listen To You

Everyone wants to be heard, to be listened to. It is not easy to find someone who will just listen to you, without talking. Most people want to talk to you as well as listen to you.

It is very healthy to talk about your thoughts, feelings, and problems and to have someone listen to them without talking very much.

Find someone who is wise who will listen to you without talking very much. This person may be someone in your family, a friend, or someone at work.

Talk to this person about the way you feel; talking about things will always help you to feel better about yourself, especially if the person you are talking to is a good listener.

## 64.

# Don't Pass On Gossip

Gossip is a bad habit. It's never very good or nice to hear gossip or to say it.

If you listen to gossip you give value to the gossip itself and value to the person who says it. This does little more than to keep the negative talk going around and around.

The thing about passing gossip to others is that you will feel bad after you have passed it on. Everyone is hurt in some way by gossip, not just the one saying it.

When it is passed on it just makes everyone feel bad.

Have the courage to say, 'I don't want to hear this' or, if you can't do that, don't pass on the gossip to other people. It will only hurt you, the person you are talking about, and the person you are saying it to.

## 65.

# Be Positive And Generous To Others

To be positive toward others is a generous thing to do. When you talk of the good things about people and tell them, they will feel good about themselves. It is a great skill to talk about the good things in others.

When you are positive when talking with someone, you will also feel better about yourself.

It is very easy to meet someone and to look them up and down and notice the things that you think are wrong with them. However, it is a valuable skill to look them up and down and notice the good things in them.

The more you do this, the more you will be able to notice the good things in others and the better you will feel about yourself.

## 66.

# Do More Kind Things

Being kind to someone else always helps you to feel better about yourself.

Here are some things you can do:
- Pick up some waste others forgot or left behind.
- Tell a friend that she looks beautiful.
- Give something special to someone you know.
- Allow someone who is in a hurry to walk ahead of you.
- Open a door for someone else and smile as you do it.
- Do something pleasant for someone without them knowing.
- Help someone do something that is difficult for them.
- Phone your parent/parents.
- Be kind to someone to whom it is hard for you to be kind.
- Tell your friends you care for them.
- Be kind to the people who serve you in shops.
- Next time someone speaks to you, listen to their every word.

You can be kind to others in little ways every day. There are many ways; try to think of some of your own.

## 67.

# Don't Compare Yourself With Others

It is great to have friends. However, a danger in friendships is if you compare friends with each other, or yourself with them.

Comparing yourself with another person is like comparing an apple with an orange. Both taste good, both are good for you, both have a purpose, both are of value, but not in exactly the same way.

Be yourself; you aren't exactly like anyone else in the whole world. Life is not a race to be better than others or think that you are better than someone else. Nor is it useful to think of yourself as less than others. It's not possible to measure one person against another person anyway. Everyone is of great value in their own way.

Accept your friends as they are and like them the way they are and accept and like yourself as you are.

## 68.

# Like Yourself As You Are

Do you want friendship from others, and change how you act to get that friendship? When you do this, is it a success? When you act like someone that you really aren't, or someone you think everyone else will like, you don't let your real self be seen. When you try to please what you think other people want you will probably please neither yourself nor the other person.

In reality you can never know what other people think; the best you can do is to guess.

Like yourself first, just the way you are. It will require courage to start liking yourself as you are right now. Don't wait until you lose weight, have better clothes, speak better English, or have better friendships; start liking yourself now.

Set goals for things you want to change, but accept and like yourself now!

## 69.

# Learn To Deal With Disputes

Every dispute with a friend is an option to build a better friendship. Sometimes some pain and unhappiness are necessary as a way for you to work out how you can become better friends.

Friends don't have to believe exactly the same things as you believe. Accept the ideas and beliefs your friends have that are different from yours. You can also ask them to accept your beliefs that are different from theirs.

A dispute need not break up a friendship. If you do have a dispute, make sure you talk about it carefully. Try to find a way to forgive each other and value the friendship.

## 70.

# Find Your Own Style

Have you ever gone to a party and found you are in a room full of people who all look the same, are dressed the same way, think the same thoughts, and say the same things?

Whatever the style they use, most 'in' or fashionable groups are really telling the same story. The story is that they are people who want the security of 'group thinking' where all decisions about style and image are made for them.

There may be times when you like the look of a group of people so much that you can forget who you are and what you stand for. That is part of growing up and being human.

Find your own style and image, your own way of dressing, thinking, and talking. You are special and it is good for you to show your own style no matter what your friends are doing.

## 71.

# Make A Difference To Other People

Was there a person in your life who really meant something to you and who you liked just as they were? This person might have been in your family, a friend, or a teacher. They gave you ideas that made your life better and their excitement for life made a difference to you.

You also can make a difference to other people you meet. Sometimes without even knowing it, you make a difference to others.

Remember to be open and positive when you talk with people and to listen and be kind whenever you have the chance to be. You too can have that same power with people.

*Chapter 7*

# Grow Your Talents

*'We ask ourselves: Who am I to be brilliant,
gorgeous, talented, fabulous?
Actually, who are you not to be?'*

Marianne Williamson,
Author

## 72.

# Find Your Talents

Each of you has a talent, something you do well that you are likely to discover in your lifetime. A talent is a skill, something you can do with ease and that you really enjoy doing.

It could be to write, to paint, to use computer skills, to make clothes, to talk well, to enjoy walking, to be a good swimmer; just something you like to do that you find easy to do.

Get in contact with and grow your talent. Practice doing it every day. Practice for a half an hour a day or maybe a couple of hours a week. When you practice your talent you become better at it and you increase your belief in your talent and in yourself.

## 73.

# Listen To Your Feelings

Most people are afraid to listen to their feelings and trust what they are feeling. Sometimes this is because they have been taught to believe only what they can see and not what they feel. Sometimes it is because they don't trust what they feel.

If you listen to your feelings you will be able to get in touch with your great talent or find an answer to a problem, or find the cause of stress.

When you feel fear or stress, stop and take deep breaths. Feel the stress first and then take some deep breaths and let the stress go.

To listen to your feelings, close your eyes and ask yourself, 'What is the best thing for me to do about this problem right now?' Then be quiet, breathe deeply, and wait for an idea or thought to come into your mind. Such an idea may come to you in a minute or in days but wait, it will come.

Do what you feel you need to do with that idea. Your feelings are valuable; value how you feel, and listen and act on the ideas that come from your feelings.

## 74.

# Do Something Different Every Day

Do something new and different every day.

Each day go out into the world with fresh, open eyes. Picture yourself as a child again. How did you see things when you were a child? See the world as a child does, as if there was nothing you couldn't do or achieve.

Change a usual practice. Travel in a different bus or train. Go to a different cake shop or restaurant for coffee. Read a different magazine.

Try something you always wanted to do but felt you couldn't. It doesn't have to be a big thing; it can be something quite little.

Just get started.

## 75.

# Share Your Passion

Find something for which you have a passion in your life and do it often. You will become more sure of yourself when you do things you love to do; your true light will shine through.

Passion and excitement can be included in anything you do. It can be included when you spend time with your partner, with your friends, listening to music, writing, dancing, reading, or any of the things you love to do.

When you add passion, it is like adding something special when you cook a meal. It makes the food taste better. Having a passion for doing or enjoying something in life is like adding something special to your life.

## 76.

# Find A New Interest Or Skill

Sometimes you can become very busy with your work, your relationship, your friends and family or with all three, and this can lead you to have repetitive experiences.

If you think and act differently from time to time you will grow your skills and become more valuable in the market place.

One way to get out of thinking or acting repetitively is to find a new interest or skill and to grow that. Is there something new that you would wish to learn to do?

If so, then get started. Make a list of the things you need to do and learn. This may be to buy some materials, to start to study, or to join a group with common likes.

Whatever it is, start now.

*Chapter 8*

# Care For Yourself

*'At any moment I could start being a better person —
but which moment should I choose?'*

Ashleigh Brilliant,
Author

## 77.

# Care For Yourself

Do you care for yourself well, or do you think that everyone else is more important than you and not care for yourself as well as you could?

You need to care for and be kind to yourself as well as caring for other people, and not see others as more important than you.

You can care for yourself in many ways. Think about ways you might care for yourself and write them down.

Do you like a warm bubble bath or a long shower? If so, have one often. Exercise, relax, buy yourself flowers or your favorite candy, play a game, sit in nature, look at a river, read a favorite book, climb a tree, give yourself pleasure and love for one full day. These are some of the simple things you can do to care for yourself.

Do your favorite things to care for yourself often.

## 78.

# Say 'No' When You Need To

Many people are afraid to say 'No', afraid that their partner or another person will no longer like them. Care for yourself and build your self-esteem by saying 'No' when it feels right to say it. Don't let others walk over you.

Other people will want you to do things that you don't want to do. You may say 'Yes' to please them but doing so may hurt or upset you.

When you say 'No' you show your values and what you believe. You let others know as well.

If you say 'Yes' when you really want to say 'No' you let yourself down. Have the courage to speak up and say what you really mean.

## 79.

# Let Yourself Cry Sometimes

You may believe that when you feel sad or unhappy or hurt, you should have courage and not show how you are feeling. In some situations it may be wise to protect yourself by not showing how you feel but mostly it is better for you to accept your feelings. It is OK to show that you are happy or pleased or delighted; equally, it is OK to show that you are angry or sad or unhappy.

It is healthy to cry now, just as it was healthy to cry when you were a baby.

Those who don't know how to cry with their whole heart don't really know how to laugh well either.

## 80.

# Be Careful About What You Read

Some magazines are not healthy to read. Magazines about rich or famous people only make you feel unhappy because you come to think your life is not as good as theirs.

When you buy these magazines, you allow the publishers to treat you as a person who should live their life like a famous person not like yourself.

Such magazines don't talk about your inner beauty or your strengths. Don't read them or, if you do read them, read them as comic books, for fun only. Most of the articles about famous people are not even true, but they can make you feel bad about yourself.

Read positive magazines and books. Good-quality books which help you to learn and understand yourself and others. Pass the time with magazines that have beautiful pictures in them.

You must choose the images you want to have in your mind.

## 81.

# Turn Off The TV, Turn On Your Music

Choose what you will watch on TV and what you will not watch. Do not have the TV turned on all the time, as your mind will accept the messages from it even if you do not think you are hearing it.

When you watch the news too much, you see in a short time much of the really bad things that have happened in the world, and very little that is positive. This can make you feel negative about life. You can control how much of this negative news you see; the best method is to switch it off.

So turn on the TV only for things you choose to watch; turn on your music for pleasure and read a newspaper for information.

When you listen to music, it talks to your heart and creates positive ideas in your mind. Music has a way of filling us with love. It isn't important which type of music you listen to; listen to whatever you like. Music creates a space for love and understanding.

## 82.

# Clear Out Your Wardrobe

How long is it since you cleared out your wardrobe?

Clean out all the clothes that don't fit you any more. Give away or throw out any old clothes that you haven't worn for a year and you know you will never use again.

When you clean out old things in your life that you don't use any more, this is the same as cleaning out your mind.

When you clean out the old things, whether that is clothing or old thoughts, you can then move forward into the future feeling clear and sure, with space for new thoughts and new feelings to take the place of the old ones.

## 83.

# Think Before You Buy: Do You Really Need This?

Do you shop for things you feel you need, but you don't really have the money to pay for? Or do you buy things just because they are fashionable, and will make you feel good, even if you do not really need them or you do not really have the money?

Does your shopping for dresses or shoes or handbags use money that you could use for good food, or a better home, or a holiday?

Addiction to shopping or to fashion can be as real as an addiction to cigarettes or eating too much food. Whether you are dealing with an addiction to cigarettes, food, or to shopping, the answer is the same. You need to think about your actions, what you do and why you do it, and what you need to do to change your actions.

It is a good start to accept that you have a problem, and then you can plan what you will do to change your addictive habits.

## 84.

# Like Your Body Now

Do you like the way you look or do you think you should be taller or prettier or thinner or have a different body?

If you don't like yourself now because of the way you look, you may not like yourself any better if you were able to change your weight or hair color.

Learn to like all the good things about yourself now. Write down a list of all the things that you like about yourself. Look at this list and learn to like yourself as you are right now.

The things you like about yourself may be:

| | | | |
|---|---|---|---|
| walk well | weight | hair | nose |
| eyes | height | feet | mouth |
| smile | clear skin | relaxed | health |
| body language | eyebrows | dress well | neck |

In the future you may want to change something about your body, such as how much you weigh or your hair color. If so, you can set goals to change these things, but accept and like yourself as you are now.

*Chapter 9*

# Make Time For Relaxation

*'Every now and then go away,
have a little relaxation,
for when you come back to your work
your judgment will be surer;
since to remain constantly at work
will cause you to lose power of judgment . . . . '*

Leonardo da Vinci,
Artist, inventor, scientist

## 85.

# Make Time For Yourself

Do you allow time for yourself? Do you have times where you do something just for you? This may not feel natural because most of us believe that our value is in doing things such as work and things around the home.

Sometimes we believe our value is in doing things for others. But whether you are a student, a mother, a worker, a wife, a world leader, a sportsperson, or a busy person, allowing time for yourself is good for you.

Give yourself some pleasure and fun or just some quiet time alone. You are worthy of pleasure and fun and need to make this part of your life. You are also worthy of some quiet time just for you.

Make some time for yourself, every day. Doing this improves your sense of worth. Take time to do something for yourself that you really enjoy.

## 86.

# Be Calm

Many people worry too much about the future. Do you feel or do any of the following?
- Worry about things you can do nothing about.
- Feel negative a lot of the time.
- Feel too worried about your work.
- Don't want to mix with friends or meet new people.
- Don't eat well.
- Feel stressed.
- Feel really worried about the future.

Here are some things you can do:
- Train your mind to look at the good things that happen around you, not just the negative things.
- Change things in small steps; decide to do one small thing at a time and be happy to do that.
- Talk to someone you trust about your feelings and fears.
- Write in a notebook about how you feel.
- Take up yoga to still your mind.
- Get out into the fresh air and walk; create good feelings in your body.
- Think mostly about today, the present moment, rather than worrying about the future.
- Be kind to yourself.

## 87.

# Learn To Breathe Deeply

To breathe is something we all do every moment of our lives. It's easy. We don't have to think about it; it just happens. Most of us breathe short breaths, in and out, but when we do this we do not care for ourselves as well as we might. Breathing more deeply more often is very good for you.

Try this. Lie down, put a book on your stomach and another on your chest. Take a breath. If the book on your chest rises higher than the one on your stomach you are not breathing as deeply as you could.

When you breathe deeply you will become calmer and you will clear your mind when you feel upset or worried.

To breathe deeply is to care for your body and care for yourself better.

## 88.

# Learn To Relax

It is not always easy to learn how to relax. Learning how to relax and doing so will help you feel well and happy. Relaxing also helps to relieve stress.

Ideas for relaxing your body:
- Lie down with your back straight.
- Uncross your arms and legs.
- Close your eyes.
- Take some deep breaths, hold each breath for a couple of seconds and let it go.
- Allow your body to relax.
- Think about each part of your body in turn and let go of any stress there.

You can have thoughts but try not to think thoughts that worry or stress you. Your arms and legs will feel heavy. Now you can enjoy being relaxed and calm.

Try to stay that way for at least five minutes and do this once or twice every day.

## 89.

# Do Often What You Like To Do

When you often do what you enjoy doing this will help you to rest, relax, and feel good about yourself.

Whatever you like to do, do it often. Read, walk, play sport, draw a picture, day dream, play or listen to music. It doesn't matter how big or small your interest is, just do it often.

Doing things you like to do will help you to feel better about yourself. This will help you to go to work feeling good about yourself. You will also find that you work better and you can add more value at work.

*Chapter 10*

# Discover How To Be Energetic

*'Whether you are smiling, laughing, feeling
enthusiasm or quiet serenity,
the energy of joy is the most powerful
motivator there is . . . . Joy calls us to live more fully.'*

Diane Dreher,
Author

## 90.

# Find Your Favorite Exercises

Exercise is a good way for the human body to feel good. Exercise allows the body a natural sense of well-being.

If you exercise every day your body will be more healthy and you will feel well and happy. You will also look and feel better in your clothes.

Exercise can be simple; you do not need to have a walking machine. You might walk up the stairs instead of using the elevator. You might walk instead of traveling by bus or train. Stretching your body or doing yoga for a half hour a day is simple exercise and very good for your body.

Decide which exercises you like and those which make you feel well and happy, and do them often.

## 91.

# Eat Right And Well

What you eat has a big part to play in how you look and feel as well as in your health. Many people want to get fit or are worried about being overweight but don't do anything to change to healthy eating.

You need to eat the right foods for your body to be in good health.

Start each day with a healthy breakfast. A healthy breakfast will help you to start the day with energy.

To eat a healthy breakfast, lunch, and dinner will nourish you well and give you energy for the whole day, especially around 3 p.m. to 4 p.m. when some people have low energy.

If you are a person who has low energy in the afternoons, eat fresh fruits, fresh vegetables, or nuts. Stay away from sweet things such as drinks with sugar, and candy.

Small, healthy meals each day will keep you well and feeling healthy.

## 92.

# Care For Your Body

A healthy body needs you to do these things:
- Eat various good foods.
- Eat with passion.
- Drink lots of water.
- Have lots of sleep.
- Relax with family and friends.
- Have some quiet time by yourself.
- Exercise often.
- Be happy most of the time, not sad.
- Believe in yourself.
- Work to make your relationships better.
- Enjoy sex often with your partner.
- Show your feelings; talk about how you feel.
- Laugh often.
- Learn to deal with your anger.
- Grow warm and loving friendships.

Be kind to your body. It is going to be your body for your whole life, so you need to look after it!

## 93.

# Drink Enough Water

Water is a key to good health and long life.

Many people have too many sweet drinks or coffee. These dry out the body and make you want more of these drinks.

Make sure that every second drink you have is a glass of water. So when you have a coffee or tea or sugar drink, make sure your next drink is a glass of water.

Same with alcohol: after each glass of alcohol have a glass of water; don't drink too much alcohol.

Sometimes give your body a rest from alcohol, coffee, and sweet drinks. Instead, have lots of water.

## 94.

# Don't Work Too Many Hours

Do you work long hours? Do you sometimes work through your lunch break or late into the night?

If you work long hours and do not rest you will suffer from stress and become very tired. Many people who work too many hours are not as useful as those who have time away from their job to do other things, and rest.

Give yourself time with your friends and family instead of working too many hours. You will find that when you do come back to your work you will be more fresh and clear about your work.

You could also decide to wake an hour earlier each morning and get to work early to allow you to come home in time to relax or spend time with family and friends.

## 95.

# Keep Your Mind Active

Think about the ways you can keep your mind active and bright. Here are some ideas:
- Read a book every week or so.
- Play games of cards, or board games.
- Think of yourself and others in the best light.
- Notice people doing things right most of the time and tell them.
- Have fun, smile, laugh, and look for positive things every day.
- Trust your feelings.
- Accept change as part of life and let change happen.
- Care for yourself as well as for others.
- Keep learning new things.
- Keep your mind open to new ideas and thoughts.

When you keep your mind busy you will also keep it healthy.

## 96.

# Create Positive Energy

Creating positive energy in your mind is something that you must do every day. It is easy to feel sad or upset about small things. Unless you control these feelings you can weaken your positive energy.

It is easy to think someone is acting badly toward you and to become sad.

The energy in your mind may be made weak or strong by how you feel and how you think. If you think positive thoughts you will create more energy.

You can sense the energy someone is sending to you. You may feel that someone doesn't like you, even though they may act very pleasant to you.

One way to keep positive energy in your mind is not to allow what other people think of you to touch your thoughts and feelings. You can never really know what other people think of you even if you can sense that it is not good.

To protect yourself, create positive energy in your mind about yourself. Be pleasant to yourself no matter what you think other people are thinking about you.

## 97.

# Think About The Things You Want

It is important to think thoughts about what you want to have in your life rather than thoughts about things you do not want in your life.

When you worry, you think about the things you do not want to happen rather than thinking about the positive things you want to happen.

It is just as easy to see positive pictures in your mind as it is to see negative pictures. Don't think about the things that could go wrong in your life. If you think about these things a lot you will build worry and feel stress or anger.

Think positively about the present and future; this will help you to create a positive, happy life.

## 98.

# Choose Positive Words

'I am.' These are the two words that come before most of your self talk.

Instead of saying things such as 'I am bad at English', 'I am tired', and 'I am scared' say, 'I am learning English well', 'I am well', 'I am strong enough to try this.'

People who are good at sport are very careful about their self talk and always use 'I am' followed by positive words about what they want to do.

A woman who has won many gold medals for swimming told me she talked to herself as she swam up and down the pool in practice. She repeated words that told her mind how she wanted to swim. 'I am fast' and 'I am strong' were some of the words she chose.

Think like a sportsperson; say things that create positive self talk.

## 99.

# Be A Person Who Takes Action

Don't be a 'wait and see' person. Be an action person. Live your life with energy every day. When you need to decide, do so with the best information you have at the time and go forward firmly with positive energy.

People who 'wait and see' all their lives miss so many chances for trying new things, learning new things, and living life well.

Don't be influenced too much by what other people tell you to do. Do what excites you and be in control of what happens in your life.

People who have a high level of self-esteem are active people who make decisions about their lives.

## 100.

# Break Through Your Fear

Try new and different thoughts and actions often. You should often try new things you haven't done before.

Do you sometimes think you would love to do something different or try something you have never tried before but a little voice inside of you says, 'Don't do it'? That little voice is just trying to keep you safe but it often stops you from trying new things and things of interest to you.

Break through the fears you have about trying new thoughts and actions. Try something new every day. To do so may worry you but you will learn so much that will be of value and you will become a more interesting and a happier person.

# Postscript

There are many thoughts and ideas in this book, all about ways that you can take greater responsibility for your life and create a happier and more enjoyable future in which your dreams and desires may come true for you.

Please, do not feel because there are so many suggestions in this book, that there is much that is wrong or bad about you or needs to be changed. Do not feel that there is so much to do that you are afraid to start. Please do not try to do too much, too quickly.

Remember that you are a wonderful, able, interesting person who has much that is good and successful in your life. There may be some things that you would like to change or improve: this book gives you some ideas about how to change or improve these things. The changes you may want to make are only a small part of the whole you.

We hope you enjoy your journey of discovery, creation, happiness, and love. Be kind to yourself on your journey.

Vicki Bennett and Ian Mathieson

# Word List

- LEVEL 1、2は本文で使われている全ての語を掲載しています。
  LEVEL 3以上は、中学校レベルの語を含みません。ただし、本文で特殊な意味で使われている場合、その意味のみを掲載しています。
- 語形が規則変化する語の見出しは原形で示しています。不規則変化語は本文中で使われている形になっています。
- 一般的な意味を紹介していますので、一部の語で本文で実際に使われている品詞や意味と合っていないことがあります。
- 品詞は以下のように示しています。

| 名名詞 | 代代名詞 | 形形容詞 | 副副詞 | 動動詞 | 助助動詞 |
| 前前置詞 | 接接続詞 | 間間投詞 | 冠冠詞 | 略略語 | 俗俗語 |
| 熟熟語 | 頭接頭語 | 尾接尾語 | 記記号 | 関関係代名詞 |

## A

- □ **a** 冠 ①1つの、1人の、ある ②〜につき
- □ **able** 形 ①《be - to 〜》(人が) 〜することができる ②能力のある
- □ **about** 副 ①およそ、約 ②まわりに、あたりを 前 ①〜について ②〜のまわりに[の] **How about 〜?** 〜はどうですか。〜しませんか。 **What about 〜?** 〜についてあなたはどう思いますか。〜はどうですか。
- □ **above** 前 ①〜の上に ②〜より上で、〜以上で ③〜を超えて 副 ①上に ②以上に 形 上記の 名《the −》上記の人[こと]
- □ **absorb** 動 ①吸収する ②《be -ed in 〜》〜に夢中である
- □ **accept** 動 ①受け入れる ②同意する、認める
- □ **achieve** 動 成し遂げる、達成する、成功を収める
- □ **achievement** 名 ①達成、成就 ②業績
- □ **act** 名 行為、行い 動 ①行動する ②機能する ③演じる
- □ **action** 名 ①行動、活動 ②動作、行為 ③機能、作用 **take action** 行動をとる
- □ **active** 形 ①活動的な ②積極的な ③活動[作動]中の
- □ **activity** 名 活動、活気
- □ **actually** 副 実際に、本当に、実は
- □ **add** 動 ①加える、足す ②足し算をする ③言い添える
- □ **addiction** 名 ①(麻薬などの) 常用、中毒 ②(物事に) ふけること、熱中 **addiction to 〜** 〜への依存症
- □ **addictive** 形 中毒性の、常習的な
- □ **advance** 名 進歩、前進 **in advance** 前もって 動 進む、進める、進歩する[させる] **advance one's career** 出世する
- □ **advanced** 動 advance (進む) の過去、過去分詞 形 上級の、先に進んだ、高等の
- □ **advice** 名 忠告、助言、意見
- □ **afraid** 形 ①心配して ②恐れて、こわがって **I'm afraid (that) 〜** 残念ながら〜、悪いけれど〜
- □ **after** 前 〜の後に[で]、〜の次に **after all** 結局 **After you.** どうぞお先に。 **one after another** 次々に 副 後に[で] 接 (〜した) 後に[で]
- □ **afternoon** 名 午後
- □ **afterward** 副 その後、のちに

118

# WORD LIST

- **again** 副再び、もう一度
- **against** 前①~に対して、~に反対して、(規則など)に違反して ②~にもたれて
- **agree** 動①同意する ②意見が一致する
- **ahead** 副①前方へ[に] ②前もって ③進歩して、有利に go ahead 先に行く、《許可を表す》どうぞ
- **air** 名①《the -》空中、空間 ②空気、《the -》大気 ③雰囲気、様子
- **alcohol** 名アルコール
- **all** 形すべての 代全部、すべて(のもの[人]) not ~ at all 少しも[全然]~ない 名全体 副まったく、すっかり all right よろしい、申し分ない
- **allow** 動①許す、《- ~ to …》~が…するのを可能にする、~に…させておく ②与える
- **alone** 形ただひとりの 副ひとりで、~だけで
- **along** 前~に沿って 副前へ、ずっと、進んで along the way これまでに get along やっていく、はかどる
- **already** 副すでに、もう
- **also** 副~も(また)、~も同様に 接その上、さらに
- **although** 接~だけれども、~にもかかわらず、たとえ~でも
- **always** 副いつも、常に not always ~ 必ずしも~であるとは限らない
- **am** 動~である、(~に)いる[ある] 《主語がIのときのbeの現在形》
- **a.m.** 《A.M.とも》午前
- **an** 冠①1つの、1人の、ある ②~につき
- **and** 接①そして、~と… ②《同じ語を結んで》ますます ③《結果を表して》それで、だから and so on ~など
- **anger** 名怒り

- **angry** 形怒って、腹を立てて
- **another** 形①もう1つ[1人]の ②別の 代①もう1つ[1人] ②別のもの one another お互いに
- **answer** 動①答える、応じる ②《- for ~》~の責任を負う 名答え、応答、返事
- **any** 形①《疑問文で》何か、いくつかの ②《否定文で》何も、少しも(~ない) ③《肯定文で》どの~も 代①《疑問文で》(~のうち)何か、どれか、誰か ②《否定文で》少しも、何も[誰も]~ない ③《肯定文で》どれも、誰でも if any もしあれば、あったとしても 副少しは、少しも
- **anyone** 代①《疑問文・条件節で》誰か ②《否定文で》誰も(~ない) ③《肯定文で》誰でも
- **anything** 代①《疑問文で》何か、どれでも ②《否定文で》何も、どれも(~ない) ③《肯定文で》何でも、どれでも anything but ~ ~のほかは何でも、少しも~でない 副いくらか
- **anyway** 副①いずれにせよ、ともかく ②どんな方法でも
- **appearance** 名①現れること、出現 ②外見、印象
- **apple** 名リンゴ
- **are** 動~である、(~に)いる[ある] 《主語がyou, we, theyまたは複数名詞のときのbeの現在形》名アール《面積単位。100平方メートル》
- **area** 名①地域、地方、区域、場所 ②面積
- **arm** 名①腕 ②腕状のもの、腕木、ひじかけ ③《-s》武器、兵器 動武装する[させる]
- **around** 副①まわりに、あちこちに ②およそ、約 go around and around in one's mind (思考などが)心の中をグルグルと回る 前~のまわりに、~のあちこちに
- **article** 名①(法令・誓約などの)箇条、項目 ②(新聞・雑誌などの)記事、論文

## Signposts For Balance In Love And Work

- **artist** 名 芸術家
- **as** 接 ①《as ～ as …の形で》…と同じくらい～ ②～のとおりに、～のように ③～しながら、～しているときに ④～するにつれて、～にしたがって ⑤～なので ⑥～だけれども ⑦～する限りでは **as ～ as one can** できる限り ～ **as for ～** ～はどうかというと **as if [though] ～** まるで～のように **as long as ～** ～する限りは、～の間(は) **as to ～** ～については、～に応じて **as well as …** …はもちろん～も、～も…も 前 ①～として(の) ②～の時 副 同じくらい 代 ①～のような ②～だが
- **Ashleigh Brilliant** アシュレイ・ブリリアント《アメリカの作家》
- **aside** 副 わきへ[に]、離れて **set aside time to ～** ～する時間をつくる
- **ask** 動 ①尋ねる、聞く ②頼む、求める **ask for help** 助けを求める
- **assist** 動 手伝う、列席する、援助する
- **at** 前 ①《場所・時》～に[で] ②《目標・方向》～に[を]、～に向かって ③《原因・理由》～を見て[聞いて・知って]
- **author** 名 著者、作家 動 著作する、創作する
- **away** 副 離れて、遠くに、去って、わきに 形 離れた、遠征した 名 遠征試合

### B

- **baby** 名 ①赤ん坊 ②《呼びかけで》あなた 形 ①赤ん坊の ②小さな
- **back** 名 ①背中 ②裏、後ろ 副 ①戻って ②後ろへ[に] 形 裏の、後ろの
- **bad** 形 ①悪い、へたな ②気の毒な ③(程度が)ひどい、激しい **That's too bad.** 残念だ。
- **badly** 副 ①悪く、まずく、へたに ②とても、ひどく
- **balance** 名 ①均衡、平均、落ち着き ②てんびん ③残高、差額 動 釣り合いをとる
- **basis** 名 ①土台、基礎 ②基準、原理 ③根拠 ④主成分
- **bath** 名 入浴、風呂 動 入浴する[させる]
- **be** 動 ～である、(～に)いる[ある]、～となる 助 ①《現在分詞とともに用いて》～している ②《過去分詞とともに用いて》～される、～されている
- **beautiful** 形 美しい、すばらしい 間 いいぞ、すばらしい
- **beauty** 名 ①美、美しい人[物] ②《the -》美点
- **because** 接 (なぜなら)～だから、～という理由[原因] **because of ～** ～のために、～の理由で
- **become** 動 ①(～に)なる ②(～に)似合う ③becomeの過去分詞
- **bed** 名 ①ベッド、寝所 ②花壇、川床、土台 **go to bed** 床につく、寝る
- **bedroom** 名 寝室
- **bedtime** 名 就寝の時刻 **bedtime exercise** 寝る前の体操
- **been** 動 be (～である)の過去分詞 助 be (～している・～される)の過去分詞
- **before** 前 ～の前に[で]、～より以前に 接 ～する前に 副 以前に
- **begin** 動 始まる[始める]、起こる
- **behind** 前 ①～の後ろに、～の背後に ②～に遅れて、～に劣って 副 ①後ろに、背後に ②遅れて、劣って
- **belief** 名 信じること、信念、信用
- **believe** 動 信じる、信じている、(～と)思う、考える
- **belong** 動《- to ～》～に属する、～のものである
- **best** 形 最もよい、最大[多]の 副 最もよく、最も上手に **best of all**

## WORD LIST

何よりも、いちばん 名《the –》①最上のもの ②全力、精いっぱい at one's best 最高の状態で at (the) best せいぜい、よくても do [try] one's best 全力を尽くす

- **better** 形 ①よりよい ②(人が)回復して 副 ①よりよく、より上手に ②むしろ had better ～ ～するほうがよい、～しなさい
- **between** 前 (2つのもの)の間に [で・の] 副 間に
- **beyond** 前 ～を越えて、～の向こうに beyond one's reach ～の手の届かない 副 向こうに
- **big** 形 ①大きい ②偉い、重要な 副 ①大きく、大いに ②自慢して
- **blame** 動 とがめる、非難する 名 ①責任、罪 ②非難
- **board** 名 ①板、掲示板 ②委員会、重役会 board game 盤ゲーム on board (乗り物などに)乗って、搭乗して 動 ①乗り込む ②下宿する
- **body** 名 ①体、死体、胴体 ②団体、組織 ③主要部、(文書の)本文
- **book** 名 ①本、書物 ②《the B-》聖書 ③《-s》帳簿 動 ①記入する、記帳する ②予約する
- **both** 形 両方の、2つとものの 副《both ～ and … の形で》～も…も両方とも 代 両方、両者、双方
- **boyfriend** 男友だち
- **break** 動 ①壊す、折る ②(記録・法律・約束を)破る ③中断する break into ～ ～に押し入る、急に～する break out 発生する、急に起こる break through ～ ～を打ち破る break up やめさせる、断ち切る、ばらばらになる、解散させる 名 ①破壊、割れ目 ②小休止 take a break ひと休みする
- **breakfast** 朝食
- **breath** 名 ①息、呼吸 ②《a –》(風の)そよぎ、気配、きざし hold the breath 息を止める take a deep breath 深呼吸する
- **breathe** 動 ①呼吸する ②ひと息つく、休息する breathe in 息を吸う breathe out 息を吐き出す
- **bright** 形 ①輝いている、鮮明な ②快活な ③利口な 副 輝いて、明るく
- **brightly** 副 明るく、輝いて、快活に
- **brilliant** 形 光り輝く、見事な、すばらしい
- **bring** 動 ①持ってくる、連れてくる ②もたらす、生じる bring about 引き起こす bring together 引き合わせる bring up 育てる
- **broken** 動 break (壊す)の過去分詞 形 ①破れた、壊れた ②落胆した
- **brought** 動 bring (持ってくる)の過去、過去分詞
- **bubble** 泡 動 泡立つ、沸き立つ bubble bath 泡風呂
- **build** 動 建てる、確立する build trust 信頼を築き上げる 名 体格、構造
- **bus** 名 バス
- **business** 名 ①職業、仕事 ②商売 ③用事 形 ①職業の ②商売上の
- **busy** 形 ①忙しい ②(電話で)話し中で ③にぎやかな、交通が激しい
- **but** 接 ①でも、しかし ②～を除いて 前 ～を除いて、～のほかは 副 ただ、のみ、ほんの
- **buy** 動 買う、獲得する 名 購入、買った[買える]物
- **by** 前 ①《位置》～のそばに[で] ②《手段・方法・行為者・基準》～によって、～で ③《期限》～までには ④《通過・経由》～を経由して、～を通って 副 そばに、通り過ぎて

## C

- **cake** 名 ①菓子、ケーキ ②固まり 動 固まる
- **call** 動 ①呼ぶ、叫ぶ ②電話をかける ③立ち寄る 名 ①呼び声、叫び ②

電話(をかけること) ③短い訪問
- **calm** 形穏やかな, 落ち着いた 名静けさ, 落ち着き 動静まる, 静める
- **can** 助①~できる ②~してもよい ③~ありうる ④《否定文で》~のはずがない Can I ~? ~してもよいですか。 Can you ~? ~してくれますか。 名缶, 容器 動缶詰[瓶詰]にする
- **candy** 名キャンディー, 甘いもの
- **card** 名①カード, 券, 名刺, はがき ②トランプ, トランプ遊び
- **care** 名心配, 注意 take care 気をつける, 注意する take care of ~ ~の世話をする, ~に気をつける, ~を処理する 動①《通例否定文・疑問文で》気にする, 心配する ②世話をする care for ~ ~を慈しむ, ~の世話をする, 《否定文・疑問文で》~を好む
- **career** 名①(生涯の・専門的な)職業 ②経歴, キャリア career goal 職業上の目的
- **careful** 形注意深い, 慎重な
- **carefully** 副注意深く, 丹念に
- **caring** 形思いやりのある
- **carry** 動①運ぶ, 連れていく, 持ち歩く ②伝わる, 伝える carry on ~ ~を続ける carry out 実行する, 成し遂げる
- **cause** 名原因, 理由, 動機 動(~の)原因となる, 引き起こす
- **chance** 名①偶然, 運 ②好機 ③見込み by any chance ひょっとして by chance 偶然 形偶然の, 思いがけない 動偶然起こる
- **change** 動①変わる, 変える ②交換する ③両替する 名①変化, 変更 ②取り替え, 乗り換え ③つり銭, 小銭
- **charge** 動①(代金を)請求する ②(~を…に)負わせる ③命じる 名①請求金額, 料金 ②責任 ③非難, 告発 in charge of ~ ~を担当して, ~の責任を負って take charge of ~ に責任を持つ
- **checkerboard** 名チェス盤 checkerboard of life 人生のチェス盤
- **chest** 名①大きな箱, 戸棚, たんす ②金庫 ③胸, 肺
- **child** 名子ども
- **choice** 名選択(の範囲・自由), え り好み, 選ばれた人[物] 形精選した
- **choose** 動選ぶ, (~に)決める choose one's words 言葉を選ぶ
- **chose** 動 choose (選ぶ)の過去
- **cigarette** 名(紙巻)たばこ
- **circle** 名①円, 円周 ②循環, 軌道 ③仲間, サークル 動回る, 囲む
- **clarify** 動①明確にする, 解明する ②浄化する
- **clean** 形①きれいな, 清潔な ②正当な 動掃除する clean out 一掃する 副①きれいに ②まったく, すっかり
- **clear** 形①はっきりした, 明白な ②澄んだ ③(よく)晴れた 動①はっきりさせる ②片づける ③晴れる clear out 片付ける 副①はっきりと ②すっかり, 完全に
- **clearly** 副①明らかに, はっきりと ②《返答に用いて》そのとおり
- **climb** 動登る, 徐々に上がる 名登ること, 上昇
- **close** 形①近い ②親しい ③狭い 副①接近して ②密集して 動①閉まる, 閉める ②終える, 閉店する
- **clothe** 動服を着せる, 《受け身形で》(~を)着ている, (~の)格好をする
- **clothes** 動 clothe (服を着せる)の3人称単数現在 名衣服, 身につけるもの
- **coffee** 名コーヒー
- **Colin Tipping** コリン・ティッピング《アメリカの作家》
- **colleague** 名同僚, 仲間, 同業者
- **color** 名①色, 色彩 ②絵の具 ③血

## Word List

色 動色をつける

- **come** 動①来る, 行く, 現れる ②(出来事が)起こる, 生じる ③~になる ④comeの過去分詞 come about 起こる come back to ~ ~へ帰ってくる come off 取れる, はずれる come one's way 遭遇する, 手に入る come true 実現する come up with ~ ~に追いつく, ~を思いつく, ~を提案する

- **comfortable** 形快適な, 心地いい

- **comic** 形喜劇の, こっけいな, おかしい 名①こっけいな人[物] ②漫画

- **common** 形①共通の, 共同の ②普通の, 平凡な ③一般の, 公共の common sense 常識 名①共有地 ②公園 in common (with ~) (~と)共通して

- **compare** 動①比較する, 対照する ②たとえる (as) compared with [to] ~ ~と比較して, ~に比べれば

- **complete** 形完全な, まったくの, 完成した 動完成させる

- **compliment** 名①賛辞, 敬意 ②《-s》あいさつ make a compliment (人) をほめる 動ほめる, お世辞を言う

- **computer** 名コンピューター

- **condition** 名①(健康)状態, 境遇 ②《-s》状況, 様子 ③条件 動適応させる, 条件づける

- **confide** 動信頼する, 信用する, (秘密などを)打ち明ける confide in ~ ~を信用する

- **consider** 動①考慮する, ~しようと思う ②(~と)みなす ③気にかける, 思いやる

- **consideration** 名①考慮, 考察 ②考慮すべきこと take ~ into consideration ~を考慮する

- **constantly** 副絶えず, いつも, 絶え間なく

- **contact** 名①接触, 交渉 ②関係, 連絡 eye contact 視線を交わすこと get in contact with ~ ~と連絡をとる 動①接触する ②連絡をとる

- **contain** 動①含む, 入っている ②(感情などを)抑える

- **continue** 動続く, 続ける, (中断後)再開する, (ある方向に)移動していく continue to ~ ~し続ける

- **control** 動①管理[支配]する ②抑制する, コントロールする 名①管理, 支配(力) ②抑制 take control of ~ ~を制する

- **cook** 動料理する, (食物が)煮える 名料理人, コック

- **could** 助①can (~できる)の過去 ②《控え目な推量・可能性・願望などを表す》Could you ~? ~してくださいますか。

- **count** 動①数える ②(~を…と)みなす ③重要[大切]である count for ~ ~の値打ちがある, ~に値する 名計算, 総計, 勘定

- **couple** 名①2つ, 対 ②夫婦, ひと組 ③数組 a couple of ~ 2, 3の~ 動つなぐ, つながる, 関連させる

- **courage** 名勇気, 度胸

- **course** 名①進路, 方向 ②経過, 成り行き ③科目, 講座 ④策, 方策 of course もちろん, 当然

- **cover** 動①覆う, 包む, 隠す ②扱う, (~に)わたる, 及ぶ ③代わりを務める 名覆い, カバー

- **coworker** 名仕事仲間

- **create** 動創造する, 生み出す, 引き起こす

- **creation** 名創造[物]

- **creative** 形創造力のある, 独創的な creative thinking 創造的思考

- **creatively** 副独創的に

- **critical** 形①批評の, 批判的な ②危機的な, 重大な critical of ~ ~に批判的で

- **cross** 動①横切る, 渡る ②じゃまする ③十字を切る cross off 線を

引いて消す 名十字架,十字形のもの
- **cry** 動泣く,叫ぶ,大声を出す,嘆く 名泣き声,叫び,かっさい
- **culture** 名①文化 ②教養 ③耕作,栽培 動耕す,栽培する

## D

- **dance** 動踊る,ダンスをする 名ダンス,ダンスパーティー
- **danger** 名危険,障害,脅威
- **date** 名①日付,年月日 ②デート 動①日付を記す ②デートする
- **day** 名①日中,昼間 ②日,期日 ③《-s》時代,生涯 **one day** ①(過去の)ある日 ②(未来の)いつか
- **daydream** 名空想,夢想
- **deal** 動①分配する ②《- with [in] ~》~を扱う,~に対処する 名①取引,扱い ②(不特定の)量,額 **a good [great] deal (of ~)** かなり[ずいぶん・大量](の~),多額(の~)
- **December** 名12月
- **decide** 動決定[決意]する,(~しようと)決める,判決を下す **decide on ~** ~を決定する
- **decision** 名①決心 ②決定,判決 ③決断(力) **make decisions about ~** ~に対して意思決定する
- **dedicated** 動 dedicate (捧げる)の過去,過去分詞 形①献身的な,熱心な ②専用の
- **deed** 名行為,行動
- **deep** 形①深い,深さ~の ②深遠な ③濃い 副深く
- **deeply** 副深く,非常に
- **delight** 動喜ぶ,喜ばす,楽しむ,楽しませる 名喜び,愉快
- **delightful** 形楽しい,愉快にさせる
- **deserve** 動(~を)受けるに足る,値する,(して)当然である
- **desire** 動強く望む,欲する 名欲望,欲求,願望
- **desk** 名①机,台 ②受付(係),フロント,カウンター,部局
- **destroy** 動破壊する,絶滅させる,無効にする
- **detail** 名①細部,《-s》詳細 ②《-s》個人情報 動詳しく述べる
- **develop** 動①発達する[させる] ②開発する
- **Diane Dreher** ダイアン・ドレイアー《アメリカの作家》
- **did** 動 do (~をする)の過去 助 do の過去
- **difference** 名違い,相違,差 **make a difference to ~** ~に影響を及ぼす
- **different** 形異なった,違った,別の,さまざまな
- **differently** 副(~と)異なって,違って
- **difficult** 形困難な,むずかしい,扱いにくい
- **difficulty** 名①むずかしさ ②難局,支障,苦情,異議 ③《-ties》財政困難
- **dinner** 名①ディナー,夕食 ②夕食[食事]会,祝宴
- **direction** 名①方向,方角 ②《-s》指示,説明書 ③指導,指揮
- **directly** 副①じかに ②まっすぐに ③ちょうど
- **disagree** 動①意見が合わない ②一致しない
- **discover** 動発見する,気づく
- **discovery** 名発見
- **dispute** 名論争,議論 **dispute with ~** ~との論争 動反論する,論争する
- **do** 動①《ほかの動詞とともに用いて現在形の否定文・疑問文をつくる》 ②《同じ動詞を繰り返す代わりに用いる》 ③《動詞を強調するのに用いる》 動~をする **do away with ~** ~を

## Word List

- 廃止する **do with** ～ ～を処理する **do without** ～ ～なしですませる
- □ **does** 動 do (～をする) の 3 人称単数現在 助 do の 3 人称単数現在
- □ **done** 動 do (～をする) の過去分詞
- □ **door** 名 ①ドア, 戸 ②一軒, 一戸
- □ **doubt** 疑い, 不確かなこと 動 疑う
- □ **down** 副 ①下へ, 降りて, 低くなって ②倒れて 前 ～の下方へ, ～を下って 形 下方の, 下りの
- □ **draw** 動 ①引く, 引っ張る ②描く ③引き分けになる[する]
- □ **dream** 名 夢, 幻想 **the man of your dreams** 理想の男性 動 (～の) 夢を見る, 夢想[想像]する
- □ **dress** 名 ドレス, 衣服, 正装 動 ①服を着る[着せる] ②飾る
- □ **drink** 動 飲む, 飲酒する 名 飲み物, 酒, 1 杯
- □ **drive** 動 ①車で行く, (車を) 運転する ②追いやる, (ある状態に) する 名 ドライブ
- □ **dry** 形 ①乾燥した ②辛口の 動 乾燥する[させる], 干す **dry out** 乾かす
- □ **during** 前 ～の間 (ずっと)

### E

- □ **each** 形 それぞれの, 各自の 代 それぞれ, 各自 **each other** お互いに 副 それぞれに
- □ **early** 形 ①(時間や時期が) 早い ②初期の, 幼少の, 若い 副 ①早く, 早めに ②初期に, 初めのころに
- □ **ease** 名 安心, 気楽 **with ease** 簡単に 動 安心させる, 楽にする, ゆるめる
- □ **easily** 副 ①容易に, たやすく, 苦もなく ②気楽に
- □ **easy** 形 ①やさしい, 簡単な ②気楽な, くつろいだ **take it easy** 気楽にやる
- □ **eat** 動 食べる, 食事する **eat right** 正しい食事をする **eat well** 正しい食事をとる
- □ **effect** 名 ①影響, 効果, 結果 ②実施, 発効 **in effect** 有効な, 事実上 動 もたらす, 達成する
- □ **effort** 名 努力 (の成果) **put effort into** ～ ～に取り組む
- □ **eighty** 名 80 (の数字), 80 人[個] 形 80 の, 80 人[個] の
- □ **either** 形 ①(2 つのうち) どちらかの ②どちらでも 代 どちらも, どちらでも 副 ①どちらか ②《否定文で》 ～もまた (…ない) 接《either ～ or …の形で》 ～かまたは…か
- □ **Eleanor Roosevelt** エレノア・ルーズヴェルト《アメリカの社会運動家》
- □ **elevator** 名 エレベーター
- □ **else** 副 ①そのほかに[の], 代わりに ②さもないと **or else** さもないと
- □ **email** 名 電子メール, E メール 動 (人) に電子メールを送る, メールで (人) に～を送る
- □ **emotion** 名 感激, 感動, 感情
- □ **empty** 形 ①空の, 空いている ②(心などが) ぼんやりした, 無意味な 動 空になる[する], 注ぐ
- □ **end** 名 ①終わり, 終末, 死 ②果て, 末, 端 ③目的 **in the end** とうとう, 最後には 動 終わる, 終える
- □ **energetic** 形 エネルギッシュな, 精力的な, 活動的な
- □ **energy** 名 ①力, 勢い ②元気, 精力, エネルギー
- □ **English** 名 ①英語 ②《the –》英国人 形 ①英語の ②英国 (人) の
- □ **enjoy** 動 楽しむ, 享受する **enjoy oneself** 楽しく過ごす, 楽しむ
- □ **enjoyable** 形 楽しめる, 愉快な
- □ **enjoyment** 名 楽しむこと, 喜び

- **enough** 形 十分な, (〜するに)足る 名 十分(の量[数]), たくさん **enough of** 〜 〜はもうたくさん 副 (〜できる)だけ, 十分に, まったく **cannot** 〜 **enough** いくら〜してもしたりない
- **enthusiasm** 名 情熱, 熱意, 熱心
- **equal** 形 等しい, 均等な, 平等な 動 匹敵する, 等しい 名 同等のもの[人]
- **equally** 副 等しく, 平等に
- **escape** 動 逃げる, 免れる, もれる 名 逃亡, 脱出, もれ
- **especially** 副 特別に, とりわけ
- **even** 副 ①《強意》〜でさえも, 〜ですら, いっそう, なおさら ②平等に **even if** 〜 たとえ〜でも **even though** 〜 〜であるのに, たとえ〜でも 形 ①平らな, 水平の ②等しい, 均一の ③落ち着いた 動 平らになる[する], 釣り合いがとれる
- **event** 名 出来事, 事件, イベント **at all events** ともかく, いずれにしても **in any event** 何が起ころうとも
- **ever** 副 ①今までに, これまで, かつて ②《強意》いったい
- **every** 形 ①どの〜も, すべての, あらゆる ②毎〜, 〜ごとの **every now and then** しばしば
- **everybody** 代 誰でも, 皆
- **everyone** 代 誰でも, 皆
- **everything** 代 すべてのこと[もの], 何でも, 何もかも
- **exactly** 副 ①正確に, 厳密に, ちょうど ②まったくそのとおり
- **example** 名 例, 見本, 模範 **for example** たとえば
- **except** 前 〜を除いて, 〜のほかは **except for** 〜 〜を除いて, 〜がなければ 接 〜ということを除いて
- **exchange** 動 交換する, 両替する 名 ①交換, 両替 ②小切手, 為替
- **excite** 動 興奮させる, 刺激する
- **excitement** 名 興奮(すること)
- **exercise** 名 ①運動, 体操 ②練習 動 ①運動する, 練習する ②影響を及ぼす
- **expect** 動 予期[予測]する, (当然のこととして)期待する
- **experience** 名 経験, 体験 動 経験[体験]する
- **eye** 名 ①目, 視力 ②眼識, 観察力 ③注目 **eye contact** 視線を交わすこと **keep an eye on** 〜 〜から目を離さない
- **eyebrow** 名 まゆ(眉)

## F

- **fabulous** 形 すばらしい, すてきな, 途方もない
- **face** 名 ①顔, 顔つき ②外観, 外見 ③(時計の)文字盤, (建物の)正面 **face to face** 面と向かって, 差し向かいで **in (the) face of** 〜 〜の面前で, 〜に直面して 動 直面する, 立ち向かう
- **fact** 名 事実, 真相 **in fact** 実は, 要するに
- **fail** 動 ①失敗する, 落第する[させる] ②《-to 〜》〜し損なう, 〜できない ③失望させる **never [not] fail to** 〜 必ず〜する 名 失敗, 落第点
- **fair** 形 ①正しい, 公平[正当]な ②快晴の ③色白の, 金髪の ④かなりの 副 ①公平に, きれいに ②見事に
- **Faith Hope** フェイス・ホープ《アフリカで活動するオーストラリアの作家・宣教師》
- **fall** 動 ①落ちる, 倒れる ②(値段・温度が)下がる ③(ある状態に)急に陥る **fall in love** 恋に落ちる 名 ①落下, 墜落 ②滝 ③崩壊 ④秋
- **family** 名 家族, 家庭, 一門, 家柄
- **famous** 形 有名な, 名高い

# WORD LIST

- **fashion** 名①流行, 方法, はやり ②流行のもの(特に服装)
- **fashionable** 形①流行の ②上流社会の
- **fast** 形①(速度が)速い ②(時計が)進んでいる ③しっかりした 副①速く, 急いで ②(時計が)進んで ③しっかりと, ぐっすりと
- **fast-forward** 名①急速な前進, 速やかな進歩 ②早送り 動①急速に前進する ②早送りする
- **fat** 形①太った ②脂っこい ③分厚い 名脂肪, 肥満
- **fault** 名①欠点, 短所 ②過失, 誤り **at fault** 誤って, 非難されるべき **find fault with ~** ~のあら探しをする 動とがめる
- **favorite** 名お気に入り(の人[物]) 形お気に入りの, ひいきの
- **fear** 名①恐れ ②心配, 不安 動①恐れる ②心配する
- **feel** 動感じる, (~と)思う **feel bad** 不愉快に思う **feel easy** 気を楽にする **feel for ~** ~に同情する, ~を手さぐりで探す **feel good about oneself** 自分がいい気分になる **feel like ~** ~がほしい, ~したい気がする, ~のような感じがする **feel right** 正しいと感じる **feel upset** 気を悪くする
- **feet** 名①foot(足)の複数 ②フィート《長さの単位。約30cm》
- **fellow** 名①仲間, 同僚 ②人, やつ 形仲間の, 同士の **fellow worker** 同僚
- **felt** 動feel(感じる)の過去, 過去分詞 名フェルト 形フェルト(製)の
- **feminist** 名フェミニスト, 男女同権主義者
- **fill** 動①満ちる, 満たす ②《be -ed with ~》~でいっぱいになる
- **find** 動①見つける ②(~と)わかる, 気づく, ~と考える ③得る
- **fine** 形①元気な ②美しい, りっぱな, 申し分ない ③晴れた ④細かい, 微妙な 副りっぱに, 申し分なく 動罰金を科す 名罰金
- **finish** 動終わる, 終える 名終わり, 最後
- **firm** 形堅い, しっかりした, 断固とした 副しっかりと
- **firmly** 副しっかりと, 断固として
- **first** 名最初, 第一(の人[物]) **at first** 最初は, 初めのうちは 形①第一の, 最初の ②最も重要な 副第一に, 最初に **first of all** 何よりもまず
- **fit** 形①適当な, 相応な ②体の調子がよい **get fit** 体を鍛える 動合致[適合]する, 合致させる 名発作, けいれん, 一時的興奮
- **five** 名5(の数字), 5人[個] 形5の, 5人[個]の
- **fix** 動①固定する[させる] ②修理する ③決定する ④用意する, 整える
- **flower** 名①花, 草花 ②満開 動花が咲く
- **follow** 動①ついていく, あとをたどる ②(~の)結果として起こる ③(忠告などに)従う ④理解できる
- **food** 名食物, えさ, 肥料
- **for** 前①《目的・原因・対象》~にとって, ~のために[の], ~に対して ②《期間》~間 ③《代理》~の代わりに ④《方向》~へ(向かって) 接というわけは~, なぜなら~だから
- **force** 名力, 勢い 動①強制する, 力ずくで~する, 余儀なく~させる **force ... to ~** …に~することを強いる ②押しやる, 押し込む
- **forget** 動忘れる, 置き忘れる
- **forgive** 動許す, 免除する
- **forgot** 動forget(忘れる)の過去, 過去分詞
- **forgotten** 動forget(忘れる)の過去分詞
- **forward** 形①前方の, 前方へ向かう ②将来の ③先の 副①前方に ②将来に向けて ③先へ, 進んで **go**

- forward 前進する look forward to ~[~ing] ~を期待する move forward 前進する 動①転送する ②進める 名前衛
- **found** 動 find (見つける)の過去, 過去分詞
- **fresh** 形①新鮮な, 生気のある ②さわやかな, 清純な ③新規の
- **friend** 名 友だち, 仲間
- **friendly** 形 親しみのある, 親切な, 友情のこもった 副 友好的に, 親切に
- **friendship** 名 友人であること, 友情
- **from** 前 ①《出身・出発点・時間・順序・原料》~から ②《原因・理由》~がもとで
- **fruit** 名 ①果実, 実 ②《-s》成果, 利益 動 実を結ぶ
- **full** 形①満ちた, いっぱいの, 満期の ②完全な, 盛りの, 充実した 名全部
- **fully** 副 十分に, 完全に, まるまる
- **fun** 名 楽しみ, 冗談, おもしろいこと make fun of ~ ~をからかう 動 からかう, ふざける
- **future** 名 未来, 将来 in the future 将来は 形 未来の, 将来の

## G

- **gain** 動 ①得る, 増す ②進歩する, 進む 名 ①増加, 進歩 ②利益, 得ること, 獲得
- **game** 名 ゲーム, 試合, 遊び, 競技 動 賭けごとをする
- **gave** 動 give (与える)の過去
- **generous** 形 ①寛大な, 気前のよい ②豊富な
- **gentle** 形 ①優しい, 温和な ②柔らかな
- **get** 動 ①得る, 手に入れる ②(ある状態に)なる, いたる ③わかる, 理解する ④~させる ⑤(ある場所に)達する, 着く get on with ~ ~と仲良く[うまく]やっていく get over 克服する, 乗り越える get started 始める
- **gift** 名 ①贈り物 ②(天賦の)才能 動 授ける
- **Gita Bellin** ギタ・ベリン《オーストラリアの形而上学者》
- **give** 動 ①与える, 贈る ②伝える, 述べる ③(~を)する give away ただで譲る give in 降参する, (書類などを)提出する give off 発散する, 放つ give out 配する, 発表する, 尽きる give up あきらめる, やめる
- **given** 動 give (与える)の過去分詞 形 与えられた
- **giving** 形 寛大な
- **glad** 形 ①うれしい, 喜ばしい ②《be-to ~》~してうれしい, 喜んで~する
- **glass** 名 ①ガラス(状のもの), コップ, グラス ②鏡, 望遠鏡 ③《-es》めがね a glass of ~ コップ1杯の~
- **go** 動 ①行く, 出かける ②動く ③進む, 経過する, いたる ④(ある状態に)なる be going to ~ ~するつもりである go about ~ ~に取りかかる go by 経過する, 通り過ぎる go for ~ ~に出かける, ~を取りに行く, ~を好む go off 立ち去る, 発射する go on 続く, 続ける, 進んでいく go with ~ ~と一緒に行く, ~と調和する go without ~ ~なしですませる
- **goal** 名 ①目的(地), 目標 ②決勝点, ゴール set goals 目標を設定する
- **gold** 名 金, 金貨, 金製品, 金色 形 金の, 金製の, 金色の
- **gone** 動 go (行く)の過去分詞 形 去った, 使い果たした
- **good** 形 ①よい, 上手な, 優れた ②(数量・程度が)かなりの, 相当な as good as ~ ~も同然で, ほとんど~ be good at ~ [~ing] ~が得意である 間 よかった, わかった, よろしい 名 善, 徳, 益, 幸福

## Word List

- **goodness** 图①善良さ, よいところ ②優秀 ③神《婉曲表現》
- **good-quality** 形良質の
- **gorgeous** 形華麗な, 豪華な, 華やかな, すばらしい
- **gossip** 图うわさ話, ゴシップ 動うわさ話をする, 雑談する
- **grandparent** 图祖父母
- **great** 形①大きい, 広大な, (量や程度が)たいへんな ②偉大な, 優れた ③すばらしい, おもしろい
- **group** 图集団, 群 動集まる
- **grow** 動①成長する, 育つ, 育てる ②増大する, 大きくなる, (次第に～に)なる
- **guess** 動①推測する, 言い当てる ②(～と)思う **Guess what.** あのね。何だと思う？ 知ってるかい？ 图推定, 憶測
- **guidance** 图案内, 手引き
- **guide** 動(道)案内する, 導く 图①ガイド, 手引き, 入門書 ②案内人
- **guilty** 形有罪の, やましい **feel guilty** 罪悪感を感じる
- **gym** 图①体育館, ジム ②体育

## H

- **habit** 图習慣, 癖, 気質 **be in the habit of ～ing** ～する習慣がある
- **had** 動 have (持つ)の過去, 過去分詞 助 haveの過去《過去完了の文をつくる》 **had better ～** ～するほうがよい, ～しなさい
- **hair** 图髪, 毛
- **half** 图半分 形半分の, 不完全な 副半分, なかば, 不十分に
- **hand** 图①手 ②(時計の)針 ③援助の手, 助け **at hand** 近くに, すぐ使えるように **in hand** 自分の意のままに **on the other hand** 他方では 動手渡す **hand in** 差し出す, 提出する **hand out** 配る **hand over** 引き渡す, 譲渡する
- **handbag** 图ハンドバッグ
- **happen** 動①(出来事が)起こる, 生じる ②偶然[たまたま]～する
- **happiness** 图幸せ, 喜び
- **happy** 形幸せな, うれしい, 幸運な, 満足して
- **hard** 形①堅い ②激しい, むずかしい ③熱心な, 勤勉な ④無情な, 耐えがたい 副①一生懸命に ②激しく ③堅く
- **has** 動 have (持つ)の3人称単数現在 助 haveの3人称単数現《現在完了の文をつくる》
- **hate** 動嫌う, 憎む, (～するのを)いやがる 图憎しみ
- **have** 動①持つ, 持っている, 抱く ②(～が)ある, いる ③食べる, 飲む ④経験する, (病気に)かかる ⑤催す, 開く **have to ～** ～しなければならない **have to do with** ～ ～と関係がある 助《〈have + 過去分詞〉の形で現在完了の文をつくる》～した, ～したことがある, ずっと～している
- **he** 代彼は[が]
- **health** 图健康(状態), 衛生, 保健 **in good health** 健康で
- **healthy** 形健康な, 健全な, 健康によい
- **hear** 動聞く, 聞こえる **hear from ～** ～から手紙[電話・返事]をもらう **hear of ～** ～について聞く **I hear (that) ～** ～だそうだ
- **heard** 動 hear (聞く)の過去, 過去分詞
- **heart** 图①心臓, 胸 ②心, 感情, ハート ③中心, 本質 **at heart** 心底では, 実際は **by heart** 暗記して **open one's heart** 心を打ち明ける **with all one's heart** 真心を込めて, 心から **with one's whole heart** 心から
- **heavy** 形重い, 激しい, つらい
- **height** 图①高さ, 身長 ②《the -》

絶頂, 真っ盛り ③高台, 丘
- **held** 動 hold (つかむ) の過去, 過去分詞
- **help** 動 ①助ける, 手伝う ②給仕する cannot [can't] help ~ing [but ~] ~せずにはいられない help oneself 自分で取って食べる [飲む] 名助け, 手伝い
- **helpful** 形 役に立つ, 参考になる
- **helpless** 形 無力の, 自分ではどうすることもできない
- **her** 代 ①彼女を [に] ②彼女の
- **here** 副 ①ここに [で] ②《- is [are] ~》ここに~がある ③さあ, そら Here it is. はい, どうぞ。 Here we are. さあ着きました。 Here you are. はい, どうぞ。 Look here. ほら。ねえ。 名ここ
- **herself** 代 彼女自身
- **high** 形 ①高い ②気高い, 高価な 副 ①高く ②ぜいたくに 名 高い所
- **him** 代 彼を [に]
- **his** 代 ①彼の ②彼のもの
- **history** 名 歴史, 経歴
- **hit** 動 ①打つ, なぐる ②ぶつける, ぶつかる ③命中する ④(天災などが)襲う, 打撃を与える ⑤hitの過去, 過去分詞 hit on [upon] ~ ~を思いつく 名 ①打撃 ②命中 ③大成功
- **hold** 動 ①つかむ, 持つ, 抱く ②保つ, 持ちこたえる ③収納できる, 入れることができる ④(会などを)開く hold on to ~ ~に執着する, ~をしっかりと持つ 名 ①つかむこと, 保有 ②支配 [理解] 力
- **holiday** 名 祝祭日, 休暇 形 ①休日 [休暇] の ②よそ行きの, 楽しい
- **home** 名 ①家, 自国, 故郷, 家庭 ②収容所 at home 在宅して, 気楽に, くつろいで 副 家に, 自国へ 形 家の, 家庭の, 地元の 動 ①家 [本国] に帰る ②(飛行機などを) 誘導する
- **honest** 形 ①正直な, 誠実な, 心から ②公正な, 感心な
- **honestly** 副 正直に
- **honor** 名 ①名誉, 光栄, 信用 ②節操, 自尊心 in honor of ~ ~に敬意を表して, ~を記念して 動 尊敬する, 栄誉を与える
- **honorable** 形 ①尊敬すべき, 立派な ②名誉ある ③高貴な
- **hope** 名 希望, 期待, 見込み in the hope of ~ ~を望んで [期待して] 動 望む, (~であるようにと) 思う I hope (that) ~ ~だと思う, ~だとよいと思う
- **hopeless** 形 ①希望のない, 絶望的な ②勝ち目のない
- **hour** 名 1時間, 時間
- **how** 副 ①どうやって, どれくらい, どんなふうに ②なんて (~だろう) ③《関係副詞》~する方法 How do you like ~? ~はどう思いますか。~はいかがですか。 how to ~ どのように~すべきか, ~する方法
- **however** 副 たとえ~でも 接 けれども, だが
- **human** 形 人間の, 人の 名 人間 human being 人, 人間
- **humankind** 名 (種としての) 人類, 人間
- **hurry** 動 急ぐ, 急がせる, あわてる hurry up 急ぐ, 急がせる 名 急ぐこと, 急ぐ必要
- **hurt** 動 傷つける, 痛む, 害する 名 傷, けが, 苦痛, 害
- **hurtful** 形 傷つける, 有害な
- **husband** 名 夫

# I

- **I** 代 私は [が]
- **Ian Mathieson** イアン・マシソン《オーストラリアの作家・ビジネスコンサルタント》
- **idea** 名 考え, 意見, アイデア, 計画

## WORD LIST

- **if** 接 もし~ならば, たとえ~でも, ~かどうか **if any** もしあれば, あったとしても 名 疑問, 条件, 仮定
- **image** 名 ①印象, 姿 ②画像, 映像 動 心に描く, 想像する
- **imagine** 動 想像する, 心に思い描く
- **important** 形 重要な, 大切な, 有力な
- **improve** 動 改善する[させる], 進歩する
- **in** 前 ①《場所・位置・所属》~(の中)に[で・の] ②《時》~(の時)に[の・で], ~後(に), ~の間(に) ③《方法・手段》~で ④~を身につけて, ~を着て ⑤~に関して, ~について ⑥《状態》~の状態で 副 中へ[に], 内へ[に] 形 今流行の
- **include** 動 含む, 勘定に入れる
- **increase** 動 増加[増強]する, 増やす, 増える 名 増加(量), 増大 **on the increase** 増加して
- **influence** 名 影響, 勢力 動 影響をおよぼす
- **information** 名 ①情報, 通知, 知識 ②案内(所), 受付(係)
- **inner** 形 ①内部の ②心の中の **inner beauty** 内面の美しさ
- **inside** 名 内部, 内側 **inside out** 裏返しに, ひっくり返して 形 内部[内側]にある 副 内部[内側]に 前 ~の内部[内側]に
- **instead** 副 その代わりに **instead of ~** ~の代わりに, ~をしないで
- **interest** 名 ①興味, 関心 ②利害(関係), 利益 ③利子, 利息 動 興味を起こさせる
- **Internet** 名 《the -》インターネット
- **into** 前 ①《動作・運動の方向》~の中へ[に] ②《変化》~に[へ]
- **introduction** 名 紹介, 導入
- **inventor** 名 発明者, 発案者
- **is** 動 be (~である)の3人称単数現在
- **issue** 名 ①問題, 論点 ②発行物 ③出口, 流出 **at issue** 論争中の, (意見が)一致しない 動 ①(~から)出る, 生じる ②発行する
- **it** 代 ①それは[が], それを[に] ②《天候・日時・距離・寒暖などを示す》
- **its** 代 それの, あれの
- **itself** 代 それ自体, それ自身

## J

- **job** 名 仕事, 職 **do [make] a good job** うまくやってのける **Good job!** よくやった。
- **join** 動 ①一緒になる, 参加する ②連結[結合]する, つなぐ **join in ~** ~に加わる, 参加する 名 結合
- **journey** 名 ①(遠い目的地への)旅 ②行程 **go on a journey** 旅をする
- **joy** 名 喜び, 楽しみ
- **judge** 動 判決を下す, 裁く, 判断する, 評価する 名 裁判官, 判事, 審査員
- **judgment** 名 ①判断, 意見 ②裁判, 判決
- **jump** 動 ①跳ぶ, 跳躍する, 飛び越える, 飛びかかる ②(~を)熱心にやり始める 名 ①跳躍 ②急騰, 急転
- **just** 形 正しい, もっともな, 当然な 副 ①まさに, ちょうど, (~した)ばかり ②ほんの, 単に, ただ~だけ ③ちょっと

## K

- **keep** 動 ①とっておく, 保つ, 続ける ②(~を…に)しておく ③飼う, 養う ④経営する ⑤守る **keep off ~** ~を避ける **keep on ~ [~ing]** ~し続ける, 繰り返し~する **keep out** 外にいる, さえぎる, 締め出す

- **keep to ~** ～から離れない, ～を守る  **keep up** 続ける, 続く, 維持する, (遅れないで)ついていく
- **key** 名 ①かぎ, 手がかり  **key to ~** ～の手掛かり ②調子 動 かぎをかける
- **kind** 形 親切な, 優しい  **be kind enough to ~** 親切にも～する 名 種類  **kind of (~)** ある程度, いくらか, ～のような物[人]
- **kindness** 名 親切(な行為), 優しさ
- **know** 動 ①知っている, 知る, (～が)わかる, 理解している ②知り合いである  **know better (than ~)** (～より)もっと分別がある  **Who knows?** 誰にわかるだろうか。誰にもわからない。 **you know** ご存知のとおり, そうでしょう
- **knowledge** 名 知識, 理解, 学問

## L

- **lack** 動 不足している, 欠けている  **lack for ~** ～がなくて困る 名 不足, 欠乏
- **language** 名 言語, 言葉, 国語, ～語, 専門語
- **late** 形 ①遅い, 後期の ②最近の ③《the-》故～ 副 ①遅れて, 遅く ②最近まで, 以前
- **later** 形 もっと遅い, もっと後の 副 後で, 後ほど  **later on** もっと後で, のちほど  **sooner or later** 遅かれ早かれ
- **laugh** 動 笑う 名 笑い(声)
- **lead** 動 ①導く, 案内する ②(生活を)送る 名 ①鉛 ②先導, 指導
- **leader** 名 指導者, リーダー
- **learn** 動 学ぶ, 習う, 教わる, 知識[経験]を得る  **learn from ~** ～から学ぶ
- **learnt** 動 learn(学ぶ)の過去, 過去分詞
- **least** 形 いちばん小さい, 最も少ない 副 いちばん小さく, 最も少なく 名 最小, 最少  **at least** 少なくとも
- **leave** 動 ①出発する, 去る ②残す, 置き忘れる ③(～を…の)ままにしておく ④ゆだねる  **leave behind** ～を置き去りにする 名 ①休暇 ②許可 ③別れ
- **lecturer** 名 講演者, 講師
- **left** 名 《the-》左, 左側 形 左の, 左側の 副 左に, 左側に 動 leave(出発する)の過去, 過去分詞
- **leg** 名 ①脚, すね ②支柱
- **Leonardo da Vinci** レオナルド・ダ・ヴィンチ《イタリアの画家。医学や建築など多分野で活躍したルネサンス期の偉人》
- **less** 形 ～より小さい[少ない] 副 ～より少なく, ～ほどでなく  **less and less ~** だんだん少なく～, ますます～でなく  **no less than ~** ～と同じだけの, ～も同然  **not less than ~** ～以下ではなく, ～にまさるとも劣らない 名 より少ない数[量・額]
- **lessen** 動 (物・事を)少なく[小さく]する, 減らす
- **lesson** 名 授業, 学科, 課, 稽古
- **let** 動 (人に～)させる, (～するのを)許す, (～をある状態に)する  **let down** 失望させる  **let go of ~** ～から手を放す  **Let me see.** ええと。
- **level** 名 ①水平, 平面 ②水準 形 ①水平の, 平たい ②同等[同位]の 動 ①水平にする ②平等にする
- **lie** 動 ①うそをつく ②横たわる, 寝る ③(ある状態に)ある, 存在する 名 うそ, 詐欺
- **life** 名 ①生命, 生物 ②一生, 生涯, 人生 ③生活, 暮らし, 世の中
- **lifetime** 名 ①一生, 生涯 ②寿命
- **light** 名 光, 明かり 動 火をつける, 照らす, 明るくする 形 ①明るい ②(色が)薄い, 淡い ③軽い, 容易な 副 軽く, 容易に

## Word List

- **like** 動好む, 好きである would like ~ ~がほしい would like to ~ ~したいと思う Would you like ~? ~はいかがですか。前~に似ている, ~のような feel like ~ ~のように感じる, ~がほしい look like ~ ~のように見える, ~に似ている 形似ている, ~のような 接あたかも~のように 名①好きなもの ②《the[one's]–》同じようなもの[人]

- **likely** 形①ありそうな, (~)しそうな ②適当な 副たぶん, おそらく

- **list** 名名簿, 目録, 一覧表 動名簿[目録]に記入する

- **listen** 動《– to ~》~を聞く, ~に耳を傾ける

- **listener** 名聞く人, ラジオ聴取者

- **little** 形①小さい, 幼い ②少しの, 短い ③ほとんど~ない, 《a –》少しはある 名少し(しか), 少量 little by little 少しずつ 副全然~ない, 《a –》少しはある

- **live** 動住む, 暮らす, 生きている 形①生きている, 生きた ②ライブの, 実況の 副生で, ライブで

- **lives** 名life (生命) の複数

- **lock** 名錠(前) 動錠を下ろす, 閉じ込める, 動けなくする be locked into ~ ~を余儀なくされる

- **long** 形①長い, 長期の ②《長さ・距離・時間などを示す語句を伴って》~の長さ[距離・時間]の 副長い間, ずっと no longer ~ もはや~でない[~しない] not ~ any longer もはや~でない[~しない] so [as] long as ~ ~する限りは 名長い期間 before long 間もなく, やがて 動切望する, 思い焦がれる

- **long-lasting** 形長続きしている

- **look** 動①見る ②(~に)見える, (~の)顔つきをする ③注意する ④《間投詞のように》ほら, ねえ look after ~ ~の世話をする, ~に気をつける look down on ~ ~を見下す look for ~ ~を探す look into the future 未来を見る look on 傍観する, 眺める 名①一見, 目つき ②外観, 外見, 様子

- **lose** 動①失う, 迷う, 忘れる ②負ける, 失敗する

- **lot** 名①くじ, 運 ②地所, 区画 ③たくさん, たいへん, 《a – of ~, -s of ~》たくさんの~ ④やつ, 連中

- **Louise L. Hay** ルイーズ・L・ヘイ《アメリカの作家》

- **love** 名愛, 愛情, 思いやり in love with ~ ~に恋して love cannot see 恋は盲目 動愛する, 恋する, 大好きである

- **loving** 形愛に満ちた

- **low** 形①低い, 弱い ②低級の, 劣等な 副低く 名①低い水準[点] ②低速ギア

- **lunch** 名昼食, ランチ, 軽食 lunch break 昼休み

## M

- **machine** 名機械, 仕掛け, 機関

- **mad** 形①気の狂った ②逆上した, 理性をなくした ③ばかげた ④(~に)熱狂[熱中]して, 夢中の go mad 発狂する

- **made** 動make (作る) の過去, 過去分詞 形作った, 作られた

- **magazine** 名①雑誌, 定期刊行物

- **make** 動①作る, 得る ②行う, (~に)なる ③(~を…)する, (~を…)させる make do with ~ ~で間に合わせる make it 到達する, 成功する make out ~ ~を作成する, 理解する make up ~ ~を構成[形成]する make up for ~ ~の埋め合わせをする

- **man** 名男性, 人, 人類

- **manner** 名①方法, やり方 ②態度, 様子 ③《-s》行儀, 作法, 生活様式

- **many** 形多数の, たくさんの 代多

数(の人[物])
- **map** 名地図 動①地図を作る ②計画を立てる
- **Marianne Williamson** マリアンヌ・ウィリアムソン《アメリカの作家》
- **mark** 名①印,記号,跡 ②点数 ③特色 動①印[記号]をつける ②採点する ③目立たせる
- **market** 名市場,マーケット,取引,需要 market place 市場 動市場に出す
- **marry** 動結婚する
- **material** 形①物質の,肉体的な ②不可欠な,重要な 名材料,原料
- **matter** 名物,事,事件,問題 as a matter of course 当然のこと as a matter of fact 実際は no matter how ~ どんなに~であろうとも no matter what ~ たとえ何が~であろうとも 動《主に疑問文・否定文で》重要である
- **may** 助①~かもしれない ②~してもよい,~できる May I ~? ~してもよいですか。
- **maybe** 副たぶん,おそらく
- **me** 代私を[に]
- **meal** 名①食事 ②ひいた粉,あらびき粉
- **mean** 動①意味する ②(~のつもりで)言う,意図する ③~するつもりである I mean つまり,そうではなく 形①卑怯な,けちな,卑しい ②中間の 名中間,中位
- **meant** 動 mean(意味する)の過去,過去分詞
- **measure** 動①測る,(~の)寸法がある ②評価する 名①寸法,測定,計量,単位 ②程度,基準
- **medal** 名メダル
- **meet** 動①会う,知り合いになる ②合流する,交わる ③(条件などに)達する,合う meet with ~ ~に出会う
- **member** 名一員,メンバー
- **men** 名 man(男性)の複数
- **message** 名伝言 get the message (人の)真意をつかむ 動メッセージで送る,伝える
- **metaphysician** 名形而上学者
- **method** 名①方法,手段 ②秩序,体系
- **might** 助《mayの過去》①~かもしれない ②~してもよい,~できる 名力,権力
- **mind** 名①心,精神 ②知性 make up one's mind 決心する mind's eye 想像力 set one's mind to ~ ~に全力を傾ける 動①気にする,いやがる ②気をつける,用心する Never mind. 心配するな。
- **mindset** 名物の見方,思考態度
- **minute** 名①(時間の)分 ②ちょっとの間 Just [Wait] a minute. ちょっと待って。 形ごく小さい,細心の
- **miss** 動①失敗する,免れる,~を見逃す,(目標を)はずす ②(~が)ないのに気づく,(人が)いなくてさびしく思う 名はずれ,失敗
- **mistake** 名誤り,誤解,間違い by mistake 誤って 動間違える,誤解する
- **mix** 動①混ざる,混ぜる ②(~を)一緒にする mix with ~ ~と交際する 名混合(物)
- **moment** 名①瞬間,ちょっとの間 ②(特定の)時,時期 at any moment いつ何時,今にも at the moment 今は in a moment ただちに
- **money** 名金,通貨 make money 金をもうける
- **more** 形①もっと多くの ②それ以上の,余分の 副もっと,さらに多く,いっそう more and more ますます more or less 多少,多かれ少なかれ no more もう~ない no more than ~ たった~,ほんの~ not any more もう~ない once

## Word List

- **more** もう一度 **the more ~, the more …** ~すればするほどますます… 代もっと多くの物[人]
- **morning** 名朝, 午前
- **most** 形①最も多い ②たいていの, 大部分の 代①大部分, ほとんど ②最多数, 最大限 **at (the) most** せいぜい, 多くても **make the most of ~** ~を最大限利用する 副最も(多く) **most of all** とりわけ, 中でも **most of the time** 大体の場合
- **mostly** 副主として, 多くは, ほとんど
- **mother** 名母, 母親
- **motivator** 名動機付けの要因
- **mouth** 名①口 ②言葉, 発言
- **move** 動①動く, 動かす ②感動させる ③引っ越す, 移動する 名①動き, 運動 ②転居, 移動
- **movie** 名映画, 映画館
- **much** 形(量・程度が)多くの, 多量の **as much ~ as …** …と同じだけの~ 副①とても, たいへん ②《比較級・最上級を修飾して》ずっと, はるかに 名多量, たくさん, 重要なもの **as much as ~** ~と同じだけ
- **music** 名音楽, 楽曲
- **must** 助①~しなければならない ②~に違いない 名絶対に必要なこと[もの]
- **my** 代私の
- **myself** 代私自身

## N

- **nameless** 形匿名の, 無名の, 名もない
- **natural** 形①自然の, 天然の ②生まれつきの, 天性の ③当然な **it is natural for … to ~** …が~するのは当然だ
- **nature** 名①自然(界) ②天性, 性質 ③自然のまま, 実物 ④本質 **by nature** 生まれつき
- **necessary** 形必要な, 必然の **if necessary** もし必要ならば 名《-ries》必要品, 必需品
- **neck** 名首, (衣服の)えり
- **need** 動(~を)必要とする, 必要である 助~する必要がある 名①必要(性), 《-s》必要なもの ②まさかの時 **in need** 必要で, 困って
- **negative** 形①否定的な, 消極的な, ネガティブな ②負の, マイナスの, (写真が)ネガの 名①否定, 反対 ②ネガ, 陰画, 負数, マイナス
- **neither** 形どちらの~も…でない 代(2者のうち)どちらも~でない 副《否定文に続いて》~も…しない **neither ~ nor …** ~でもなく…でもない
- **never** 副決して[少しも]~ない, 一度も[二度と]~ない **never too late to ~** ~するのに遅すぎるということはない
- **new** 形①新しい, 新規の ②新鮮な, できたての **What's new?** お変わりありませんか
- **newspaper** 名新聞(紙)
- **next** 形①次の, 翌~ ②隣の 副①次に ②隣に **next to ~** ~の隣の, ~の次に 代次の人[もの]
- **nice** 形すてきな, よい, きれいな, 親切な **Nice to meet you.** お会いできてうれしい。
- **night** 名夜, 晩
- **no** 副①いいえ, いや ②少しも~ない 形~がない, 少しも~ない, ~どころでない, ~禁止 名否定, 拒否
- **nor** 接~もまたない **neither ~ nor …** ~も…もない
- **normal** 形普通の, 平均的な, 標準的な 名平常, 標準, 典型
- **nose** 名鼻, 嗅覚, におい
- **not** 副~でない, ~しない **not (~) at all** まったく(~で)ない **not ~ but …** ~ではなくて… **not yet** ま

だ～してない

- **note** 名①メモ, 覚え書き ②注釈 ③注意, 注目 ④手形 動①書き留める ②注意[注目]する

- **notebook** 名ノート, 手帳

- **nothing** 代何も～ない[しない] **for nothing** ただで, 無料で, むだに **have nothing to do with ～** ～と何の関係もない **nothing but ～** ただ～だけ, ～にすぎない, ～のほかは何も…ない

- **notice** 名①注意 ②通知 ③公告 動①気づく, 認める ②通告する

- **nourish** 動栄養を与える, 養う

- **now** 副①今(では), 現在 ②今すぐに ③では, さて **right now** 今すぐに, たった今 名今, 現在 今のところ **for now** 当分の間, 当面は **from now on** 今後 形今の, 現在の

- **nut** 名木の実, ナッツ

## O

- **objectively** 副客観的に

- **of** 前①《所有・所属・部分》～の, ～に属する ②《性質・特徴・材料》～の, ～製の ③《部分》～のうち ④《分離・除去》～から

- **off** 副①離れて ②はずれて ③止まって ④休んで 形①離れて ②季節はずれの ③休みの 前～を離れて, ～をはずれて, (値段が)～引きの

- **offer** 動申し出る, 申し込む, 提供する 名提案, 提供

- **often** 副しばしば, たびたび

- **OK** 形《許可・同意・満足などを表して. O.K.とも》よろしい, 正しい 名許可, 承認 動オーケー[承認]する

- **old** 形①年取った, 老いた ②～歳の ③古い, 昔の 名昔, 老人

- **on** 前①《場所・接触》～(の上)に ②《日・時》～に, ～と同時に, ～のすぐ後で ③《関係・従事》～に関して, ～について, ～して 副①身につけて, 上に ②前へ, 続けて

- **once** 副①一度, 1回 ②かつて **once in a while** たまに, 時々 **once or twice** 1～2度, 数回 **once upon a time** 昔々 名一度, 1回 **all at once** 突然 **at once** すぐに, 同時に 接いったん～すると

- **one** 名1(の数字), 1人[個] **one by one** 1つずつ, 1人ずつ 形①1の, 1人[個]の ②ある ③《the ‒ 》唯一の 代①(一般の)人, ある物 ②一方, 片方 ③～なもの

- **only** 形唯一の 副①単に, ～にすぎない, ただ～だけ ②やっと **if only ～** ～でありさえすれば **not only ～ but (also)** ～だけでなく…もまた 接ただし, だがしかし

- **open** 形①開いた, 広々とした ②公開された **open with ～** ～と真っすぐ向き合う 動①開く, 始まる ②広がる, 広げる ③打ち明ける

- **openhearted** 形心を開いた, 率直な 副心を開いて, 打ち明けて,

- **openly** 副率直に, 公然と

- **openness** 名開放, 公開

- **opportunity** 名好機, 適当な時期[状況]

- **option** 名選択(の余地), 選択可能物, 選択権

- **or** 接①～か…, または ②さもないと ③すなわち, 言い換えると

- **orange** 名オレンジ 形オレンジ色の

- **other** 形①ほかの, 異なった ②(2つのうち)もう一方の, (3つ以上のうち)残りの **every other ～** 1つおきの～ **the other day** 先日 代①ほかの人[物] ②《the ‒ 》残りの1つ 副そうでなく, 別に

- **our** 代私たちの

- **ourselves** 代私たち自身

- **out** 副①外へ[に], 不在で, 離れて ②世に出て ③消えて ④すっかり

## WORD LIST

- **out of ~** ～の外に、～から、(危険など)を脱して 形①外の、遠く離れた、②公表された 前～から外へ[に] 動①追い出す ②露呈する ③(スポーツで)アウトにする
- **outside** 名外部、外側 from the outside 外側から 形外部の、外側の 副外や、外側に 前～の外に[で・の・へ]、～の範囲を越えて
- **over** 前①～の上の[に]、～を一面に覆って ②～を越えて、～以上に、～よりまさって ③～の向こう側の[に] ④～の間 副①上に、一面に、ずっと ②終わって、すんで over and over (again) 何度も繰り返して over time やがて、自然に、時間とともに
- **overall** 形総体的な、全面的な 副全般的に見れば 名オーバーオール、作業着
- **over-excited** 形興奮しすぎの
- **overweight** 形太りすぎの、重量超過の
- **own** 形自身の 動持っている、所有する

### P

- **pain** 名①痛み、苦悩 ②《-s》骨折り、苦労 in pain 苦しんでいる 動苦痛を与える、痛む
- **paint** 動①ペンキを塗る ②(絵の具などで)描く 名塗料、ペンキ、絵の具
- **paper** 名①紙 ②新聞、論文、答案 ③《-s》書類 ④紙幣、手形
- **parent** 名親、《-s》両親
- **part** 名①部分、割合 ②役目 play a part 役目を果たす take part in ~ ～に参加する 動分ける、分かれる、別れる
- **partner** 名配偶者、仲間、同僚 動(～と)組む、提携する
- **party** 名①パーティー、会、集まり ②派、一行、隊、一味
- **pass** 動①過ぎる、通る、通り過ぎる ②(年月が)たつ ③(試験に)合格する ④手渡す pass away 亡くなる pass by そばを通り過ぎる、経過する pass on 通り過ぎる、(伝言などを)伝える pass the time ひまをつぶす 名①通過 ②入場券、通行許可 ③合格、パス
- **passion** 名情熱、(～への)熱中、激怒
- **passionate** 形情熱的な、(感情が)激しい、短気な
- **past** 形過去の、この前の 名過去(の出来事) 前《時間・場所》～を過ぎて、～を越して 副通り越して、過ぎて
- **patient** 形我慢[忍耐]強い、根気のある 名病人、患者
- **pay** 動①支払う、払う、報いる、償う ②割に合う、ペイする 名給料、報い
- **people** 名①(一般に)人々 ②民衆、世界の人々、国民、民族 ③人間
- **percent** 名パーセント、百分率
- **perfect** 形①完璧な、完全な ②純然たる 動完成する、改良[改善]する
- **perfection** 名完全、完成
- **perfectly** 副完全に、申し分なく
- **perhaps** 副たぶん、ことによると
- **person** 名①人 ②人格、人柄 in person (本人)自ら、自身で
- **personal** 形①個人の ②本人自らの ③容姿の
- **pet** 名ペット、お気に入り 形お気に入りの、愛がんの 動かわいがる
- **phone** 名電話 動電話をかける
- **pick** 動①(花・果実などを)摘む、もぐ ②選ぶ、精選する ③つつく、ついて穴をあける、ほじくり出す ④(～を)摘み取る pick out えり抜く、選び出す pick up 拾い上げる、車で迎えに行く、習得する、再開する、回復する 名①《the-》精選したもの ②選択(権) ③つつくもの、つるはし
- **picture** 名絵、写真、《-s》映画 動

描く, 想像する picture in one's mind 思い描く

- **place** 名 ①場所, 建物 ②余地, 空間 ③《one's -》家, 部屋 in place of ~ ~の代わりに take place 行われる, 起こる take the place of ~ ~に代わる, ~の代わりになる 動 ①置く, 配置する ②任命する, 任じる
- **plan** 名 計画, 設計(図), 案 動 計画する
- **plant** 名 ①植物, 草木 ②設備, プラント, 工場 動 植えつける, すえつける plant the seeds for ~ ~の素地を作る
- **play** 動 ①遊ぶ, 競技する ②(楽器を)演奏する, (役を)演じる 名 遊び, 競技, 劇
- **pleasant** 形 ①(物事が)楽しい, 心地よい ②快活な, 愛想のよい
- **please** 動 喜ばす, 満足させる 間 どうぞ, お願いします
- **pleasure** 名 喜び, 楽しみ, 満足, 娯楽 (**It's**) **my pleasure.** どういたしまして。
- **p.m.** 《P.M.とも》午後
- **poet** 名 詩人, 歌人
- **point** 名 ①先, 先端 ②点 ③地点, 時点, 箇所 ④《the-》要点 come to the point 核心に触れる on the point of ~ [~ing] まさに~しようとして point of view 視点, 観点, 考え方 starting point 出発点, 原点 to the point 要領を得た 動 ①(~を)指す ②とがらせる point out 指摘する
- **pool** 名 ①水たまり, プール ②共同出資 動 共同出資する
- **portion** 名 一部, 部分, 分け前 the best portion of ~ ~の最上の部分 動 分配する
- **positive** 形 ①積極的な, ポジティブな ②明確な, 明白な, 確信している ③プラスの, (写真が)ポジの 名 ①正数, プラス, 陽極 ②ポジ, 陽画
- **positively** 副 明確に, 確かに, 積極的に

- **possibility** 名 可能性, 見込み, 将来性
- **possible** 形 ①可能な ②ありうる, 起こりうる as ~ as possible できるだけ~ if possible できるなら
- **postscript** 名 ①(手紙の)追伸 ②(論文などの)追記, あとがき
- **power** 名 力, 能力, 才能, 勢力, 権力
- **powerful** 形 力強い, 実力のある, 影響力のある
- **practice** 名 ①実行, 実践 ②練習 ③慣例 ④(医者・弁護士などの)業務 ⑤やり方, 方法 in practice 実際上は 動 実行する, 練習[訓練]する
- **praise** 動 ほめる, 賞賛する 名 賞賛
- **prefer** 動 (~のほうを)好む, (~のほうが)よいと思う
- **prepared** 形 ①準備ができて ②調理された
- **present** 形 ①出席している, ある, いる ②現在の 名 ①《the-》現在 ②贈り物, プレゼント at present 現在は, 目下 動 ①紹介する ②現れる ③与える ④提出する, 述べる, 示す
- **pretend** 動 ①ふりをする, 装う ②あえて~しようとする
- **probable** 形 ありそうな, 有望な
- **probably** 副 たぶん, あるいは
- **problem** 名 問題, 難問 **No problem.** いいですよ。どういたしまして。問題ない。
- **program** 名 ①番組, プログラム ②計画, 予定表 動 ①番組[計画表]を作る ②(コンピューターの)プログラムを作る
- **protect** 動 保護する, 防ぐ
- **publisher** 名 出版社, 発行者
- **pull** 動 ①引く, 引っ張る ②引きつける **pull ahead** 前にでる, 抜く 名 ①引くこと ②縁故, コネ

## WORD LIST

- **purpose** 名目的, 意図, 決意 on purpose わざと, 故意に to the purpose 目的にかなって 動もくろむ, 企てる
- **put** 動①置く, のせる ②入れる, つける ③(ある状態に)する ④putの過去, 過去分詞 put aside わきに置く put away 片づける, 取っておく put off 延期する, 要求をそらす, 不快にさせる, やめさせる put up with ~ ~を我慢する

## Q

- **quality** 名①質, 性質, 品質 ②特性 ③良質
- **question** 名質問, 疑問, 問題 come into question 問題になる, 議論される in question 問題の, 論争中の 動①質問する ②調査する ③疑う
- **quickly** 副敏速に, 急いで
- **quiet** 形①静かな, 穏やかな, じっとした ②おとなしい, 無口な, 目立たない 名静寂, 平穏 動静まる, 静める
- **quite** 副①まったく, すっかり, 完全に ②かなり, ずいぶん ③ほとんど not quite まったく~だというわけではない quite[not] a few かなり多くの

## R

- **race** 名①競争, 競走 ②人種, 種族 動①競争[競走]する ②疾走する
- **raise** 動①上げる, 高める ②起こす ③~を育てる ④(資金を)調達する raise fear 不安にさせる raise doubts 疑いを引き起こす 名高める[上げる]こと, 昇給
- **rather** 副①むしろ, かえって ②かなり, いくぶん, やや ③それどころか逆に rather than ~ ~よりはむしろ would rather ~ than … …よりむしろ~したい
- **reach** 動①着く, 到着する, 届く ②手を伸ばして取る reach out to ~ ~に手を差し伸べる 名手を伸ばすこと, (手の)届く範囲
- **react** 動反応する, 対処する
- **read** 動読む, 読書する read over ~ ~に目を通す read through ~ ~を読み通す
- **readily** 副①すぐに, さっそく ②快く, 進んで
- **ready** 形用意[準備]ができた, まさに~しようとする, 今にも~せんばかりの 動用意[準備]する
- **real** 形実際の, 実在する, 本物の 副本当に
- **reality** 名現実, 実在, 真実(性) in reality 実際には turn into reality 実現する
- **really** 副本当に, 実際に, 確かに
- **reason** 名①理由 ②理性, 道理 動①推論する ②説き伏せる
- **receive** 動①受け取る, 受領する ②迎える, 迎え入れる
- **relationship** 名関係, 関連, 血縁関係
- **relax** 動①くつろぐ, くつろがせる ②ゆるめる, 緩和する
- **relaxation** 名息抜き, くつろぎ, 緩和, 弛緩
- **relaxed** 動 relax(くつろぐ, くつろがせる)の過去, 過去分詞 形①くつろいだ, ゆったりした ②ざっくばらんな
- **relaxing** 動 relax(くつろぐ, くつろがせる)の現在分詞 形①くつろがせる ②けだるい
- **relieve** 動(心配・苦痛などを)軽減する, ほっとさせる relieve stress ストレスを和らげる
- **remain** 動①残っている, 残る ②(~の)ままである[いる] 名《-s》①残り(もの) ②遺跡

## Signposts For Balance In Love And Work

- **remember** 動思い出す, 覚えている, 忘れないでいる
- **remind** 動思い出させる, 気づかせる
- **repeat** 動繰り返す 名繰り返し, 反復, 再演
- **repetitive** 形繰り返しの
- **repetitively** 副繰り返して
- **reply** 動返事[応答]する 名答え, 返事, 応答 in reply 返事として
- **require** 動①必要とする, 要する ②命じる, 請求する
- **respect** 名①尊敬, 尊重 ②注意, 考慮 with respect ていねいに 動尊敬[尊重]する
- **responsibility** 名①責任, 義務, 義理 ②負担, 責任 take responsibility for ～ ～の責任を負う
- **rest** 名①休息 ②安静 ③休止, 停止 ④《the -》残り 動①休む, 眠る ②休止する, 静止する ③(～に)基づいている ④(～の)ままである rest from ～ ～をやめる
- **restaurant** 名レストラン, 料理店, 食堂
- **result** 名結果, 成り行き, 成績 as a result その結果(として) as a result of ～ ～の結果(として) 動(結果として)起こる, 生じる, 結局～になる
- **return** 動帰る, 戻る, 返す 名①帰還, 返却 ②返answ, 報告(書), 申告 by return 折り返し in return (for ～) (～の)お返しに 形①帰りの, 往復の ②お返しの
- **revenge** 名復讐 in revenge of [for] ～ ～への復讐として 動復讐する
- **rich** 形①富んだ, 金持ちの ②豊かな, 濃い, 深い
- **right** 形①正しい ②適切な ③健全な ④右(側)の 副①まっすぐに, すぐに ②右(側)に ③ちょうど, 正確に right away すぐに right now 今すぐに, たった今, 現時点では right from the start そもそも初めから 名①正しいこと ②権利 ③《the -》右, ライト ④《the R-》右翼
- **rise** 動①昇る, 上がる ②生じる 名①上昇, 上がること ②発生 give rise to ～ ～を引き起こす
- **river** 名①川 ②(溶岩などの)大量流出
- **romance** 名恋愛(関係・感情), 恋愛[空想・冒険]小説
- **romantic** 形ロマンチックな, 空想的な 名ロマンチックな人
- **room** 名①部屋 ②空間, 余地
- **rule** 名①規則, ルール ②支配 as a rule 一般に, 原則として make it a rule to ～ ～することにしている make rules 規則を定める set rules 決まり[規定]を定める 動支配する
- **rush** 動突進する, せき立てる rush into ～ ～に突入する 名突進, 突撃, 殺到

## S

- **sad** 形①悲しい, 悲しげな ②惨めな, 不運な
- **sadness** 名悲しみ, 悲哀
- **safe** 形①安全な, 危険のない ②用心深い, 慎重な 名金庫
- **said** 動say (言う)の過去, 過去分詞
- **same** 形①同じ, 同様の ②前述の the same ～ as [that] … …と同じ(ような)～ 代《the -》同一の人[物] 名《the -》同様に
- **satisfaction** 名満足 to one's satisfaction ～が満足のいくように
- **say** 動言う, 口に出す that is to say すなわち They say ～. …ということだ。 to say nothing of ～ ～は言うまでもなく What do you say to ～? ～はいかがですか。 名言うこと, 言い分 間さあ, まあ

## Word List

- **saying** 名ことわざ 動say（言う）の現在分詞
- **scared** 動scare（こわがらせる）の過去, 過去分詞 形おびえた, びっくりした
- **school** 名①学校, 校舎, 授業（時間）②教習所, 学部 ③流派 ④群れ
- **scientist** 名（自然）科学者
- **search** 動捜し求める, 調べる 名捜査, 探索, 調査
- **second** 名①第2(の人[物])②(時間の)秒, 瞬時 形第2の, 2番の 副第2に 動後援する, 支持する
- **security** 名①安全性, 安心 ②担保, 抵当, 《-ties》有価証券
- **see** 動①見る, 見える, 見物する ②（～と）わかる, 認識する, 経験する ③会う ④考える, 確かめる, 調べる ⑤気をつける **I see.** わかりました。**Let me see.** ええと。**see ～ as …** ～を…と考える **See you (later).** ではまた。**you see** あのね, いいですか
- **seed** 名種 動種をまく
- **seek** 動捜し求める, 求める
- **seem** 動（～に）見える,（～のように）思われる
- **seen** 動see（見る）の過去分詞
- **self** 名①自己, ～そのもの ②私利, 私欲, 利己主義 ③自我
- **self-esteem** 名自尊心, うぬぼれ
- **send** 動①送る, 届ける ②手紙を出す ③（人を～に）行かせる ④《＋人［物など］＋…ing》…を（ある状態に）する **send for ～** ～を呼びにやる
- **sense** 名①感覚, 感じ ②《-s》意識, 正気, 本性 ③常識, 分別, センス ④意味 **in a sense** ある意味では **make sense** 意味をなす, よくわかる **sense of worth** 価値観 動感じる, 気づく
- **serenity** 名平静, 安らぎ
- **serious** 形①まじめな, 真剣な ②重大な, 深刻な,（病気などが）重い

- **serve** 動①仕える, 奉仕する ②（客の）応対をする, 給仕する ③（役目を）果たす, 務める, 役に立つ ④（球技で）サーブをする 名（球技で）サーブ（権）
- **set** 動①置く, 当てる, つける ②整える, 設定する ③（太陽・月などが）沈む ④（～を…の状態に）する, させる ⑤setの過去, 過去分詞 **set off** 出発する, 発射する **set to ～** ～に着手する **set up** 立てる,（テントを）張る, 創設する,（商売などを～として）始める 形①決められた, 固定した ②断固とした ③準備のできた 名①ひとそろい, セット ②受信機 ③（テニスなどの）セット ④舞台装置, セット
- **settle** 動安定する[させる], 落ち着く, 落ち着かせる **settle down** 落ち着く, 定住する, 沈下する, 静まる
- **seventy-five** 名75（の）
- **sex** 名①性, 性別, 男女 ②性交
- **share** 名①分け前, 分担 ②株 動分配する, 共有する
- **she** 代彼女は[が]
- **shine** 動①光る, 輝く ②光らせる, 磨く 名光, 輝き
- **shoe** 名《-s》靴 動（馬に）てい鉄をうつ
- **shop** 名①店, 小売店 ②仕事場 動買い物をする
- **short** 形①短い ②背の低い ③不足している **be short of ～** ～が足りない **in a short time** 一時間～に 副①手短に, 簡単に ②不足して **run short** 不足する, 切らす 名①《the-》要点 ②短編映画 ③（野球で）ショート **for short** 略して **in short** 要約すると
- **should** 助～すべきである, ～したほうがよい
- **shoulder** 名肩 動肩にかつぐ, 肩で押し分けて進む
- **show** 動①見せる, 示す, 見える ②明らかにする, 教える ③案内する **show off** 見せびらかす, 目立とうと

- する **show up** 顔を出す, 現れる 名 ①表示, 見世物, ショー ②外見, 様子
- □ **shower** 名 ①シャワー ②にわか雨, 夕立 ③《a-of ~》たくさんの~ 動 にわか雨が降る, 雨のように注ぐ
- □ **shy** 形 内気な, 恥ずかしがりの, 臆病な
- □ **side** 名 側, 横, そば, 斜面 **side by side** 並んで 形 ①側面の, 横の ②副次的な 動 (~の)側につく, 賛成する
- □ **sign** 名 ①きざし, 徴候 ②跡 ③記号 ④身振り, 合図, 看板 動 ①署名する, サインする ②合図する
- □ **signpost** 名 道標, 手がかり
- □ **simple** 形 ①単純な, 簡単な, 質素な ②単一の, 単独の ③普通の, ただの
- □ **simply** 副 ①簡単に, 単に, ただ ③まったく, 完全に
- □ **since** 接 ①~以来 ②~だから 前 ~以来 副 それ以来 **ever since** それ以来ずっと **long since** ずっと以前に
- □ **sit** 動 ①座る, 腰掛ける ②止まる ③位置する
- □ **situation** 名 ①場所, 位置 ②状況, 境遇, 立場
- □ **skill** 名 ①技能, 技術 ②上手, 熟練
- □ **skin** 名 皮膚, 皮, 革(製品) **clear skin** 透明感のある肌 動 皮をはぐ, すりむく
- □ **sleep** 動 ①眠る, 寝る ②活動しない 名 ①睡眠, 冬眠 ②静止, 不活動
- □ **slowly** 副 遅く, ゆっくり
- □ **small** 形 ①小さい, 少ない ②取るに足りない 副 小さく, 細かく
- □ **smile** 動 微笑する, にっこり笑う 名 微笑, ほほえみ
- □ **so** 副 ①とても ②同様に, ~もまた ③《先行する句・節の代用》そのように, そう **not so ~ as …** …ほど~でない **~ or so** ~かそこら, ~くらい **so as to ~** ~するように, ~するために **so ~ as to …** …するほど~で **so that ~** ~するために, それゆえに~ **so ~ that …** あまり~なので…だ 接 ①だから, それで ②では, さて **So what?** それがどうした。どうでもいいではないか。
- □ **society** 名 ①社会, 上流階級, ~界 ②協会, 団体 ③交際, 人前
- □ **soft** 形 ①柔らかい, 手ざわり[口当たり]のよい ②温和な, 落ち着いた ③(処分などが)厳しくない, 手ぬるい, 甘い
- □ **some** 形 ①いくつかの, 多少の ②ある, 誰か, 何か **some time** いつか, そのうち 副 約, およそ 代 ①いくつか ②ある人[物]たち
- □ **someone** 代 ある人, 誰か
- □ **something** 代 ①ある物, 何か ②いくぶん, 多少 **have something to do with ~** ~と関係がある
- □ **sometimes** 副 時々, 時たま
- □ **soon** 副 まもなく, すぐに, すみやかに **as soon as ~** ~するとすぐ **sooner or later** 遅かれ早かれ
- □ **sorry** 形 気の毒に[申し訳なく]思う, 残念な
- □ **soul** 名 ①魂 ②精神, 心
- □ **sound** 名 音, 騒音, 響き, サウンド 動 ①音がする, 鳴る ②(~のように)思われる, (~と)聞こえる 形 ①健全な ②妥当な ③(睡眠が)ぐっすりの 副 (睡眠が)ぐっすりと, 十分に
- □ **space** 名 ①空間, 宇宙 ②すき間, 余地, 場所, 間 動 間を空ける
- □ **speak** 動 話す, 言う, 演説する **so to speak** いわば **speak out** 正々堂々と意見を述べる, はっきり言う **speak up** 率直に話す
- □ **special** 形 ①特別の, 特殊な, 臨時の ②専門の **something special** 何か特別なもの
- □ **spend** 動 ①(金などを)使う, 消費[浪費]する ②(時を)過ごす **spend the rest of one's life** 余生を過ごす

## Word List

- **spoken** 動 speak (話す)の過去分詞 形 口語の
- **sport** 名 ①スポーツ ②《-s》競技会, 運動会 in [for] sport 冗談で
- **sportsperson** 名 スポーツ選手
- **stair** 名 ①(階段の)1段 ②《-s》階段, はしご
- **stand** 動 ①立つ, 立たせる, 立っている, ある ②耐える, 立ち向かう stand by そばに立つ, 傍観する, 待機する stand for ~ ~を表す, ~を支持する, ~を我慢する stand out 突き出る, 目立つ stand up straight 背中をシャンと伸ばす 名 ①台, 屋台, スタンド ②《the -s》観覧席 ③立つこと
- **start** 動 ①出発する, 始まる, 始める ②生じる, 生じさせる start off 出発する 名 出発, 開始
- **stay** 動 ①とどまる, 泊まる, 滞在する ②持続する, (~の)ままでいる stay away (from ~) (~から)離れている, 留守にする stay behind 居残る, 留守番をする stay on 居残る, とどまる, (電灯などが)ついたままである stay the same 同じ状態が続く stay up 起きている, 夜更かしする 名 滞在
- **steady** 形 ①しっかりした, 安定した, 落ち着いた ②堅実な, まじめな go steady 特定の相手とデートする, 恋人同士になる
- **step** 名 ①歩み, 1歩(の距離) ②段階 ③踏み段, 階段 step by step 一歩一歩, 着実に 動 歩む, 踏む
- **still** 副 ①まだ, 今でも ②それでも(なお) 形 静止した, 静かな 動 静かになる, 静める
- **stomach** 名 ①胃, 腹 ②食欲, 欲望, 好み
- **stop** 動 ①やめる, やめさせる, 止める, 止まる ②立ち止まる stop by (途中で)立ち寄る stop from ~ ing …が~するのを止める stop over 途中下車する 名 ①停止 ②停留所, 駅
- **store** 名 ①店 ②蓄え ③貯蔵庫, 倉庫 in store 蓄えて, 用意されて 動 蓄える, 貯蔵する
- **story** 名 ①物語, 話 ②(建物の)階
- **straight** 形 ①一直線の, まっすぐな, 直立[垂直]の ②率直な, 整然とした 副 ①一直線に, まっすぐに, 垂直に ②率直に 名 一直線, ストレート
- **strange** 形 ①知らない, 見[聞き]慣れない ②奇妙な, 変わった strange to say 不思議な話だが
- **strength** 名 ①力, 体力 ②長所, 強み ③強度, 濃度
- **stress** 名 ①圧力 ②ストレス ③強勢 動 ①強調する ②圧力を加える
- **stretch** 動 引き伸ばす, 広がる, 広げる 名 ①伸ばす[伸びる]こと, 広がり ②ストレッチ(運動)
- **strong** 形 ①強い, 堅固な, 強烈な ②濃い ③得意な 副 強く, 猛烈に
- **student** 名 学生, 生徒
- **study** 動 ①勉強する, 研究する ②調べる 名 ①勉強, 研究 ②書斎
- **style** 名 やり方, 流儀, 様式, スタイル out of style 流行遅れの
- **succeed** 動 ①成功する ②(~の)跡を継ぐ
- **success** 名 成功, 幸運, 上首尾
- **successful** 形 成功した, うまくいった
- **such** 形 ①そのような, このような ②そんなに, とても, 非常に such as ~ たとえば~, ~のような such as … …のような~ such ~ that … とても~なので… 代 そのような人[物] as such ~ ~など
- **suffer** 動 ①(苦痛・損害などを)受ける, こうむる ②(病気に)なる, 苦しむ, 悩む
- **sugar** 名 ①砂糖 ②甘言, お世辞 動 砂糖を入れる, 甘くする
- **suggestion** 名 ①提案, 忠告 ②気配, 暗示

## Signposts For Balance In Love And Work

- **suit** 名①スーツ, 背広 ②訴訟 ③ひとそろい, 一組 動①適合する[させる] ②似合う
- **sunset** 名日没, 夕焼け
- **sure** 形確かな, 確実な, 《be - to ~》必ず[きっと]~する, 確信して for sure 確かに make sure 確かめる, 手配する, to be sure 確かに, なるほど 副確かに, まったく, 本当に
- **surprise** 動驚かす, 不意に襲う 名驚き, 不意打ち to one's surprise ~が驚いたことに
- **swam** 動 swim (泳ぐ) の過去
- **sweet** 形①甘い ②快い ③親切な 名①《-s》甘い菓子 ②甘い味[香り], 甘いもの
- **swim** 動泳ぐ 名泳ぎ
- **swimmer** 名泳ぐ人, 水泳選手
- **switch** 名スイッチ 動①スイッチを入れる[切る] ②切り替える, 切り替わる

### T

- **take** 動①取る, 持つ ②持って[連れて]いく, 捕らえる ③乗る ④(時間・労力を)費やす, 必要とする ⑤(ある動作を)する ⑥飲む ⑦耐える, 受け入れる take after ~ ~に似る take away 撤去する, 持ち去る, 連れていく take off 脱ぐ, 離陸する, 出発する take out 取り出す, 連れ出す, 持って帰る take over 引き継ぐ, (前のものに代わって)優勢になる, 支配する take up 取り上げる, 拾い上げる, やり始める, (時間・場所を)とる 名①取得 ②捕獲
- **talent** 名才能, 才能ある人
- **talented** 形才能のある, 有能な
- **talk** 動話す, 語る, 相談する talk back 口答えする 名①話, おしゃべり ②演説 ③《the -》話題
- **tall** 形高い, 背の高い
- **taste** 名①味, 風味 ②好み, 趣味 動味がする, 味わう
- **taught** 動 teach (教える) の過去, 過去分詞
- **tea** 名①茶, 紅茶 ②お茶の会, 午後のお茶
- **teacher** 名先生, 教師
- **team** 名(競技の)組, チーム
- **tell** 動①話す, 言う, 語る ②教える, 知らせる, 伝える ③わかる I (can) tell you. 本当に。絶対に。
- **ten** 名10(の数字), 10人[個] 形10の, 10人[個]の
- **test** 名試験, テスト, 検査 動試みる, 試験する
- **than** 接~よりも, ~以上に
- **thank** 動感謝する, 礼を言う 名《-s》感謝, 謝意 thanks to ~ ~のおかげで
- **that** 形その, あの 代①それ, あれ, その[あの]人[物] ②《関係代名詞》~である… that is (to say) すなわち That's it. それだけのことだ。 接~ということ, ~なので, ~だから 副そんなに, それほど
- **the** 冠①その, あの ②《形容詞の前で》~な人々 副《- + 比較級, - + 比較級》~すればするほど…
- **their** 代彼(女)らの, それらの
- **theirs** 代彼(女)らのもの, それらのもの
- **them** 代彼(女)らを[に], それらを[に]
- **themselves** 代彼(女)ら自身, それら自身
- **then** 副その時(に・は), それから, 次に (every) now and then 時折, 時々 名その時 形その当時の
- **there** 副①そこに[で・の], そこへ, あそこへ ②《- is [are] ~》~がある[いる] 名そこ
- **these** 代これら, これ 形これらの, この

# Word List

- **they** 代 ①彼(女)らは[が], それらは[が] ②(一般の)人々は[が]
- **thin** 形 薄い, 細い, やせた, まばらな 副 薄く 動 薄く[細く]なる, 薄くする
- **thing** 名 ①物, 事 ②《-s》事情, 事柄 ③《one's -s》持ち物, 身の回り品 ④人, やつ
- **think** 動 思う, 考える
- **this** 形 ①この, こちらの, これを ②今の, 現在の 代 ①これ, この人[物] ②今, ここ
- **those** 形 それらの, あれらの in those days その当時 代 それら[あれら]の人[物]
- **though** 接 ①〜にもかかわらず, 〜だが ②たとえ〜でも 副 しかし
- **thought** 動 think (思う)の過去, 過去分詞 名 考え, 意見
- **thoughtful** 形 思慮深い, 考え込んだ
- **three** 形 3(の数字), 3人[個] 形 3の, 3人[個]の
- **through** 前 〜を通して, 〜中を[に], 〜中 副 ①通して ②終わりまで, まったく, すっかり
- **throw** 動 投げる, 浴びせる, ひっかける throw out 放出する 名 投げること, 投球
- **time** 名 ①時, 時間, 歳月 ②時期 ③期間 ④時代 ⑤回, 倍 all the time ずっと, いつも at a time 一度に, 続けざまに (at) any time いつでも at one time かつては at times 時折 behind time 遅刻して for a time しばらく for the time being 今のところは from time to time 時々 have a good time 楽しい時を過ごす in time 間に合って, やがて on time 時間どおりに Time is up. もう時間だ。 動 時刻を決める, 時間を計る
- **tire** 動 疲れる, 疲れさせる, あきる, あきさせる 名 (車の)タイヤ
- **to** 前 ①《方向・変化》〜へ, 〜に, 〜の方へ ②《程度・時間》〜まで ③《適合・付加・所属》〜に ④《 − + 動詞の原形》〜するために[の], 〜する, 〜すること
- **today** 名 今日 副 今日(で)は
- **together** 副 ①一緒に, ともに ②同時に
- **told** 動 tell (話す)の過去, 過去分詞
- **tomorrow** 名 明日 副 明日は
- **too** 副 ①〜も(また) ②あまりに〜すぎる, とても〜
- **tool** 名 道具, 用具, 工具
- **totally** 副 全体的に, すっかり
- **touch** 動 ①触れる, さわる, 〜を触れさせる ②接触する ③感動させる 名 ①接触, 手ざわり ②手法 get in touch (with 〜) (〜と)連絡を取る, (〜を)知る[見つける]
- **toward** 前 ①《運動の方向・位置》〜の方へ, 〜に向かって ②《目的》〜のために
- **train** 名 ①列車, 電車 ②(〜の)列, 連続 動 訓練する, 仕立てる
- **travel** 動 ①旅行する ②進む, 移動する[させる], 伝わる 名 旅行, 運行
- **treat** 動 ①扱う ②治療する ③おごる 名 ①おごり ②楽しみ
- **tree** 名 ①木, 樹木, 木製のもの ②系図
- **tried** 動 try (試みる)の過去, 過去分詞 形 試験済みの, 信頼できる
- **trouble** 名 ①困難, 迷惑 ②心配, 苦労 ③もめごと get into trouble 困ったことになる, トラブルに巻き込まれる in trouble 困って 動 ①悩ます, 心配させる ②迷惑をかける
- **true** 形 ①本当の, 本物の, 真の ②誠実な, 確かな come true 実現する
- **trust** 動 信用[信頼]する, 委託する 名 信用, 信頼, 委託
- **truth** 名 ①真理, 事実, 本当 ②誠実, 忠実さ to tell the truth 実は, 実を言えば

- **try** 動 ①やってみる、試みる ②努力する、努める **try on** 試着してみる **try out** 実際に試してみる 名 試み、試し

- **turn** 動 ①ひっくり返す、回転する[させる]、曲がる、曲げる、向かう、向ける ②(〜に)なる、(〜に)変える **turn around** 回転する、振り返る **turn away** 向こうへ行く、追い払う、(顔を)そむける **turn down** (音量などを)小さくする、弱くする、拒絶する **turn off** (スイッチなどを)ひねって止める、消す **turn on** (スイッチなどを)ひねってつける、出す **turn out** (明かりを)消す、追い出す、(結局〜に)なる、裏返しになる **turn over** ひっくり返る[返す]、(ページを)めくる、思いめぐらす、引き渡す 名 ①回転、曲がり ②順番 ③変化、転換 **by turns** 交替に **in turn** その結果、その反動として、順番に、交互に

- **TV** 名 テレビ
- **twice** 副 2倍、2度、2回
- **two** 名 2(の数字)、2人[個] 形 2の、2人[個]の
- **type** 名 ①型、タイプ、様式 ②見本、模様、典型 動 ①典型となる ②タイプで打つ

## U

- **ugly** 形 ①醜い、ぶかっこうな ②いやな、不快な、険悪な
- **uncross** 動 〜の交差を解く **uncross one's arms [legs]** 組んだ腕[脚]をほどく
- **understand** 動 理解する、わかる、〜を聞いて知っている **make oneself understood** 自分の言っていることをわからせる
- **understood** 動 understand(理解する)の過去、過去分詞
- **uneasy** 形 不安な、焦って

- **unexpected** 形 思いがけない、予期しない
- **unfinished** 形 終わっていない、不完全な
- **unhappiness** 名 不運、不幸
- **unhappy** 形 不運な、不幸な
- **uniform** 名 制服 形 (形・質が)同一の、一定の
- **university** 名 (総合)大学
- **unkind** 形 不親切な、意地の悪い
- **unless** 接 もし〜でなければ、〜しなければ
- **unpleasant** 形 不愉快な、気にさわる、いやな、不快な
- **unremembered** 形 記憶されていない、想起不能の
- **until** 前 〜まで(ずっと) 接 〜の時まで、〜するまで
- **up** 副 ①上へ、上がって、北へ ②立って、近づいて ③向上して、増して **be up to** 〜する力がある、〜しようとしている、〜の責任[義務]である **up and down** 上がったり下がったり、行ったり来たり、あちこちと **up to 〜** (最高)〜まで 前 ①〜の上(の方)へ、高い方へ ②(道)に沿って 形 上向きの、上りの 名 上昇、向上、値上がり **ups and downs** 浮き沈み
- **upset** 形 憤慨して 動 気を悪くさせる、(心・神経など)をかき乱す
- **us** 代 私たちを[に]
- **use** 動 ①使う、用いる ②費やす 名 使用、用途 **be of use** 役に立つ **have no use for 〜** 〜には用がない、〜に我慢できない **in use** 使用されて **it is no use 〜ing** 〜してもむだだ **make use of 〜** 〜を利用[使用]する **of no use** 使われないで
- **used** 動 《be - to 〜》〜に慣れている
- **useful** 形 役に立つ、有効な、有益な
- **usual** 形 通常の、いつもの、平常の、普通の **as usual** いつものように、相変わらず

## Word List

- **usually** 副 普通, いつも (は)

### V

- **valuable** 形 貴重な, 価値のある, 役に立つ
- **value** 名 価値, 値打ち, 価格 of value 貴重な, 価値のある 動 評価する, 値をつける
- **various** 形 変化に富んだ, さまざまの, たくさんの
- **vegetable** 名 野菜, 青物 形 野菜の, 植物(性)の
- **very** 副 とても, 非常に, まったく 形 本当の, きわめて, まさしくその
- **Vicki Bennett** ヴィッキー・ベネット《オーストラリアの作家・ビジネストレーナー》
- **view** 名 ①眺め, 景色, 見晴らし ②考え方, 意見 動 眺める
- **viewpoint** 名 見地, 観点, 見解
- **voice** 名 ①声, 音声 ②意見, 発言権 動 声に出す, 言い表す

### W

- **wait** 動 ①待つ, 《 – for ~》~を待つ ②延ばす, 延ばせる, 遅らせる ③《 – on [upon] ~》~に仕える, 給仕をする wait and see 静観する
- **wake** 動 ①目がさめる, 起きる, 起こす ②奮起する
- **walk** 動 歩く, 歩かせる, 散歩する walking machine ウォーキングマシン 名 歩くこと, 散歩
- **want** 動 ほしい, 望む, ~したい, ~してほしい 名 欠乏, 不足
- **wardrobe** 名 ①洋服だんす, ワードローブ ②洋服
- **warm** 形 ①暖かい, 温暖な ②思いやりのある, 愛情のある 動 暖まる, 暖める warm up 暖まる, ウォーミングアップする, 盛り上がる
- **warmly** 副 温かく, 親切に
- **was** 動 《be の第1・第3人称単数現在 am, is の過去》~であった, (~に)いた[あった]
- **waste** 動 浪費する, 消耗する 形 ①むだな, 余分な ②不毛の, 荒涼とした 名 ①浪費, 消耗 ②くず, 廃物 ③荒地
- **watch** 動 ①じっと見る, 見物する ②注意[用心]する, 監視する watch out 警戒[監視]する 名 ①警戒, 見張り ②腕時計
- **water** 名 ①水 ②(川・湖・海などの)多量の水 動 水を飲ませる, (植物に)水をやる
- **way** 名 ①道, 通り道 ②方向, 距離 ③方法, 手段 ④習慣 all the way ずっと, はるばる, いろいろと by the way ところで, 途中で by way of ~ ~を通って, ~経由で give way 道を譲る, 譲歩する, 負ける in no way 決して~でない in the [one's] way (~の)じゃまになって make one's way 進む, 行く, 成功する make way 道を譲る[あける] No way! とんでもない。 on the [one's] way (to ~) (~への)途中で under way 進行中で
- **we** 代 私たちは[が]
- **weak** 形 ①弱い, 力のない, 病弱な ②劣った, へたな, 苦手な
- **weaken** 動 弱くなる, 弱める
- **week** 名 週, 1週間
- **weigh** 動 ①(重さを)はかる ②重さが~ある ③圧迫する, 重荷である weigh up 比較して評価する
- **weight** 名 ①重さ, 重力 ②重荷, 負担 ③重大さ, 勢力 動 ①重みをつける ②重荷を負わせる
- **welcome** 間 ようこそ 名 歓迎 動 歓迎する 形 歓迎される, 自由に~してよい You're welcome. どういたしまして。よくいらっしゃいました。
- **well** 副 ①うまく, 上手に ②十分に,

- よく, かなり **as well** なお, その上, 同様に **~ as well as …** …と同様に~も **may well ~** ~するのももっともだ, 多分~だろう **Well done!** よくできた。圏へえ, まあ, ええと 形健康な, 適当な, 申し分ない **get well** (病気が)よくなる 名井戸

- □ **well-being** 形健康, 幸せ, 幸福, 満足のいく状態, 快適な暮らし, 安らぎ, 福祉(= welfare), 福利

- **were** 動 **be** の2人称単数・複数の過去)~であった, (~に)いた[あった]

- □ **what** 代①何が[を・に] ②《関係代名詞》~するところのもの[こと] **what comes one's way** 自分に起きることすべて **What (~) for?** 何のために, なぜ **What's up?** 何があったのですか。やあ, どうですか。形①何の, どんな ②なんと ③~するだけの 副いかに, どれほど

- □ **whatever** 代①《関係代名詞》~するものは何でも ②どんなこと[もの]が~とも ③どんな~でも ②《否定文・疑問文で》少しの~も, 何らかの

- □ **when** 副①いつ ②《関係副詞》~するところの, ~するとその時, ~するとき 接~の時, ~するとき 代いつ

- □ **whenever** 接①~するときはいつでも, ~するたびに ②いつ~しても **whenever possible** 可能ならいつでも

- □ **where** 副①どこに[で] ②《関係副詞》~するところの, そしてそこで, ~するところ ~なところに[へ], ~するところに[へ] 代①どこ[に], ~するところ ②~するところの

- □ **whether** 接~かどうか, ~かまたは…, ~であろうとなかろうと **whether ~ or …** ~であろうと…であろうと

- □ **which** 代①どちらの, どの, どれでも ②どんな~でも, そしてこの 代①どちら, どれ, どの人[物] ②《関係代名詞》~するところの

- □ **while** 接①~の間(に), ~する間(に) ②一方, ~なのに 名しばらくの間, 一定の時

- □ **who** 代①誰が[は], どの人 ②《関係代名詞》~するところの(人) **those who ~** ~する人々

- □ **whole** 形全体の, すべての, 完全な, 満~, 丸~ 名《the -》全体, 全部 **as a whole** 全体として **on the whole** 全体として見ると

- □ **whom** 代①誰を[に] ②《関係代名詞》~するところの人, そしてその人を

- □ **why** 副①なぜ, どうして ②《関係副詞》~するところの(理由) **Why don't you ~?** ~しませんか。**Why not?** どうしてだめなのですか。いいですとも。間①おや, まあ ②もちろん, なんだって ③ええと

- □ **wife** 名妻, 夫人

- □ **will** 助~だろう, ~しよう, する(つもりだ) **Will you ~?** ~してくれませんか。名決意, 意図

- □ **William Wordsworth** ウィリアム・ワーズワース《イギリスの詩人》

- □ **willing** 形①喜んで~する, ~しても構わない, いとわない ②自分から進んで行う **willing to ~** 喜んで~する

- □ **wisdom** 名知恵, 賢明(さ)

- □ **wise** 形賢明な, 聡明な, 博学の

- □ **wish** 動望む, 願う, (~であればよいと)思う 名(心からの)願い

- □ **with** 前①《同伴・付随・所属》~と一緒に, ~を身につけて, ~とともに ②《様態》~(の状態)で, ~して ③《手段・道具》~で, ~を使って

- □ **without** 前~なしで, ~がなく, ~しないで **not[never]… without ~ing** ~せずには…しない, ~すれば必ず…する

- □ **woman** 名(成人した)女性, 婦人

- □ **women** 名 **woman**(女性)の複数

- □ **won** 動 **win**(勝つ)の過去, 過去分